Danny boy

Words by Fred E. Weatherly

4

6

The lark in the clear air

Words by Sir Samuel Ferguson (1810–86)

Traditional Irish
arr. Alexander L'Estrange

This music is copyright. Photocopying is **ILLEGAL** and is **THEFT**.

hear the sweet lark sing, in the clear air of the day.

hear the sweet lark sing, in the clear air of the day.

hear the sweet lark sing in the clear air of the day.

A little slower

S. A. (opt. solo)

MEN

As I hear the sweet lark

A little slower

Slower still

rit.

(full)

sing in the clear air of the day.

in the clear air of the day.

rit. **Slower still**

The last rose of summer

Words by Thomas Moore

Traditional Irish
arr. Alexander L'Estrange

16

kin - dred, no rose - bud is nigh,___ to re - flect back her

kin - dred, no rose - bud is nigh,___ to re - flect back her

kin - dred, no___ rose - bud is nigh,___ to re - flect, to re-

20

blush - es, or___ give sigh___ for___ sigh.

blush - es, or___ give sigh___ for___ sigh.

- flect back,___ or give sigh___ for___ sigh.

25

I'll not leave thee,___ thou___ lone one, to___ pine on___ the___

BRITISH RAILWAYS

PAST and PRESENT

No 54

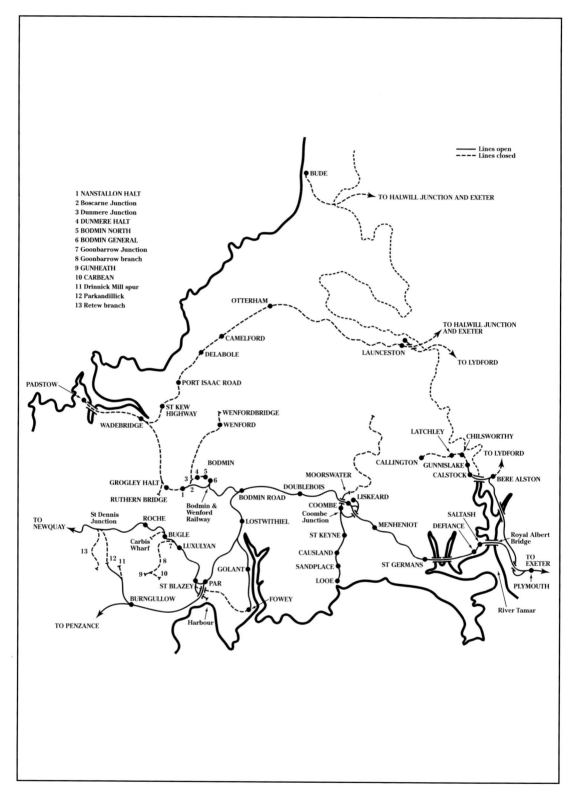

Map of the area covered by this book, showing locations featured or referred to in the text.

BRITISH RAILWAYS

PAST and PRESENT

No 54

East Cornwall

David Mitchell

Past and Present

Past & Present Publishing Ltd

First published in 2006

British Library Cataloguing in Publication Data

A catalogue record for this book is available from the British Library.

ISBN 1 85895 244 1
ISBN 978 1 85895 244 4

Past & Present Publishing Ltd
The Trundle
Ringstead Road
Great Addington
Kettering
Northants NN14 4BW

Tel/Fax: 01536 330588
email: sales@nostalgiacollection.com
Website: www.nostalgiacollection.com

Printed and bound in Great Britain

OTTERHAM: The North Cornwall Railway's westward climb to this location involved a circuitous routing around the contours at a maximum gradient of 1 in 73. The station was in a remote and exposed spot some 850 feet above sea level, a fine day allowing glimpses of the Atlantic Ocean less than 4 miles to the west. The most direct access to Otterham village, more than a mile to the north, was via a footpath. On 5 July 1961 'West Country' 'Pacific' No 34011 *Tavistock* pauses with the up 'Atlantic Coast Express'. It has just descended from the summit of the line, less than a mile to the west. The light two-coach weekday load makes an interesting comparison with the longer summer Saturday consist seen at Wadebridge only four days previously (see page 16).

The down loop was abolished and signal box closed from 7 February 1965. Since the line closed in 1966 the road bridge has been demolished and the main station building is now a dwelling, with a paddock covering part of the formation. There was also a caravan park on part of the site, but housing has replaced this in recent years. *Terry Gough/DHM*

CONTENTS

MENHENIOT station is sited on a reverse curve and serves its namesake village just over a mile to the north. On 29 July 1972 Brush Type 4 No 1960 (currently FM Rail's 47703) passes with the 1M39 0945 SO Penzance to Wolverhampton. The main chalet-style building and signal box can be noted on the down platform. The goods yard had been located to the left of the box, but this closed in 1963. Sidings were added to serve Clicker Tor Quarry in 1931, primarily for the conveyance of railway ballast, but these were taken out of use in 1969; quarry structures can be observed beyond the station building. Due to the proximity of the quarry to the line, the signalman was warned when blasting was to occur.

The signal box closed in September 1973 but survived as a permanent-way staff mess room; it is now boarded up. The station building has been demolished, but a shelter survives on the up platform. No 158741 leaves as the 1200 Penzance to Bristol Temple Meads service on 29 May 2006; this ScotRail unit was used for a couple of months on local services following First Group's take-over of the Wessex Trains franchise. *Bernard Mills/DHM*

INTRODUCTION

A lthough Cornwall is part of England, its character is quite unique, and without doubt its position as a peninsula almost separated from the rest of the country has contributed to this. Geographically it is a plateau falling chiefly towards the south. Its coast is its glory, which to the north is wild and rugged where it is battered by the broad Atlantic, its cliffs of slate and granite interspersed with magnificent surf beaches. To the south the countryside is softer and gentler, the plateau broken by the many coombs and wooded river valleys leading to the creeks and sheltered harbours on the English Channel coast.

There is also a contrast between north and south in the survival or otherwise of the Duchy's railway network. The north was once occupied by the farthest flung limbs of the London & South Western Railway's 'Withered Arm', but is now virtually devoid of all railway activity. However, not only does the former Great Western's main line through the south remain, but the Looe branch also continues to form part of the national network. Even two lines that did lose their passenger service in the 1960s survive as either a preserved railway (the Bodmin & Wenford) or a freight-only line (the Fowey branch).

Despite the vagaries and upheavals of privatisation, the HST service to London continues and direct cross-country trains are currently provided through to Glasgow and Dundee. The Newquay branch does still reach the north coast, although its existence is a somewhat schizophrenic one. On summer Saturdays through trains from London, Manchester and Newcastle bring thousands to the UK's surfing capital. However, this is at the expense of any form of service to the intermediate branch stations. For the rest of the year four trains each way have been provided daily, but their timings make it difficult to judge who exactly they are aimed at. In 2004 the outgoing Wessex Trains franchisee increased the summer weekday service to eight trains and this has continued until this year. However, the additional trains will cease according to the provisional 2007 timetable published as part of the new Greater Western franchise. The Looe service will also be cut from a regular-interval service of 13 trains a day to an irregular one of eight.

On the freight side it is pleasing to report that new business in recent years now sees cement being brought into a distribution terminal at Moorswater and scrap metal being loaded at St Blazey. However, at the time of writing china clay traffic still accounts for the bulk of freight activity within the area covered by this book. Some of the lines depicted herein would not have been built but for this industry, and the Fowey branch's continuing existence is totally dependent on it. Once there were more than 100 small producers, but eventually mergers led to the emergence of English China Clays as the dominant force in this market; this locally based company was acquired by French minerals giant Imerys in 1999. The volume of rail-borne traffic has diminished greatly over the years for a variety of reasons, including these mergers, the closure of old coal-fired kilns, new technology that allows more clay to be piped in slurry form to large central drying locations, and of course greater use of road transport. Today the impact of a global market is having a detrimental affect on the business. Just as work was being completed on this book in July 2006, it was announced that a further substantial 'rationalisation' of activity would be taking place, and the workforce within Cornwall will be reduced by more than 600 to 1400 – in an industry that once employed more than 6,000 in the county. Imerys has cited a number of reasons, including high energy costs, overseas competition and the weak dollar. It is, however, presently understood that rail will still be used for some of the remaining traffic.

I have assumed that anyone sufficiently interested in reading this book will have also seen the original Cornwall volume in the 'British Railways Past and Present' series, and I have therefore tried to complement the pictures in that title, subject of course to the availability of material. For a few locations it has been possible to take the story a little further; however, there are also places where a mundane 'present' view replicates one from the earlier book, and in a couple of instances I've included additional older views in the belief that this would be of greater interest to the reader. I hope that I am correct.

Most of the 'present' pictures were taken during September 2005 and May/June 2006 specifically for this volume. However, for the reasons stated it was often difficult to find a clay train to photograph, and I have included a number of these taken in previous years. I have also dipped into my own archive to include some views that are no longer easily accessible. It does not seem that long ago that many railwaymen were kindly disposed towards the serious enthusiast and a blind eye would often be taken when photographing from the 'wrong side of the fence'. Security and Health & Safety concerns now make this virtually impossible and unfortunately reflect the times we live in. However, in recent years I have been fortunate to partake in several official visits to both railway and china clay installations that have been organised by Cornwall railway expert Maurice Dart on behalf of the West of England branch of the RCTS, and a number of pictures have been drawn from these trips.

This is the eighth book in this series that I have been involved in, and on each occasion I have acknowledged the help received from the owners of former railway property. My visits have usually been received with at worst indifference, sometimes bemusement, but often with a degree of interest, particularly if I had photographs with me that were new to them. This time around I was refused permission to take one photograph, and this is only the second occasion that this has happened over the years. If nothing else, that one incident has reinforced my gratitude to those who have been so helpful, particularly when they have welcomed a complete stranger into their house.

As always I am also most grateful to the suppliers of photographic material, who are credited individually within, and my thanks go once more to Eric Youldon for information and comments.

David Mitchell
Exeter

BIBLIOGRAPHY

Bennett, Alan *The GWR in East Cornwall* (Runpast. 1990)

Binding, John *Brunel's Cornish Viaducts* (Pendragon, 1993)

Cooke, R. A. *Track Layout Diagrams of the GWR Section 11* (R. A. Cooke, 1977)
Atlas of the GWR (Wild Swan, 1988)

Crombleholme, R., Gibson, B., Stuckey, D. and Whetmath, C. F. D. *Callington Railways* (Forge, 1985)

Dart, Maurice *East Cornwall Mineral Railways* (Middleton, 2004)

Fairclough, Tony and Wills, Alan *Bodmin & Wadebridge* (Bradford Barton, 1979)

Gough, Terry *Cross Country Routes of the Southern* (OPC, 1983)

Gray, Peter W. *Rail Trails: South West* (Silver Link, 1992)
Steam in Cornwall (Ian Allan, 1993)

Messenger, Michael J. *Caradon and Looe* (Twelveheads, 1978)

Mitchell, David *BR Past & Present No 8 Devon* (Past & Present, 1991)

BR Past & Present No 17 Cornwall (Past & Present 1993)
BR Past & Present No 53 North & West Devon (Past & Present 2006)

Mitchell, Vic and Smith, Keith *Branch Line to Bude* (Middleton, 1996)
Branch Line to Padstow (Middleton, 1995)
Branch Lines around Bodmin (Middleton, 1996)
Wenfordbridge to Fowey (Middleton, 1998)
Plymouth to St Austell (Middleton, 2001)
Branch Line to Looe (Middleton, 1998)
Branch Lines to Newquay (Middleton, 2001)

Pryer, G. A. *Track Layout Diagrams of the SR Section 6* (R. A. Cooke, 1983)

Vaughan, John *Branches & Byways: Cornwall* (OPC, 2002)
The Newquay Branch and its Branches (OPC, 1991)

Walnutt-Read, A. *BR Steam Operating: Plymouth-Penzance* (Xpress)

Whetmath, C. F. D. *The Bodmin & Wadebridge Railway* (Town & Country, 1972)

Wroe, D. J. *The Bude Branch* (Kingfisher, 1988)
North Cornwall Railway (Irwell, 1995)

Bude branch

BUDE: Standard 3MT 2-6-2T No 82017 approaches its destination with the 9.56am train from Okehampton on 5 July 1961. This class had replaced 'M7' 0-4-4Ts on this line in 1952. Dominating the background is the gasworks, which had been much enlarged during the 1950s. The 36-lever signal box can be noted behind the front coach, and the engine is passing the 50-foot turntable, which was just long enough to accommodate a 'T9' or 'N' Class locomotive. Out of view on the right is the single-road engine shed. Running behind the turntable is the half-mile line to Bude wharf, which at one time handled much traffic, including coal and fertilisers. Until 1942 the wharf siding had connected with a narrow gauge plateway that carried sea sand used primarily as field dressing.

The wharf branch and engine shed both closed when all freight facilities on the line were withdrawn from 7 September 1964. As pictured in July 2005, this area is now occupied commercially. Some concrete railway fencing survives behind this field of view. *Terry Gough/DHM*

BUDE: Services to the town commenced on 10 August 1898, after the LSWR had extended the line from the previous terminus at Holsworthy. This extension was about 10 miles long, about half of which was in neighbouring Devon – Bude was the only Cornish station, and other stations on the line are featured in 'BR Past & Present' Nos 8 and 53. The new terminus was more than 228 miles from Waterloo and was provided with a 570-foot-long main platform (No 1) and a shorter bay platform (No 2). 'N' Class 2-6-0 No 31836 is in the latter on 5 July 1961 with the 7.02pm to Halwill, the last up train of the day. The train comprises a pair of Maunsell coaches, a former LMS luggage van and a box van; the latter vehicles conveyed mail traffic and would be taken forward from Halwill on a North Cornwall service. The goods shed can be noted to the right of the 'Mogul', while the line in the left foreground leads to the engine shed.

The passenger service ceased from 3 October 1966, and a housing estate now covers the station area. *Terry Gough/DHM*

North Cornwall Railway

LAUNCESTON: The railway reached this ancient market town in June 1865 when the Launceston & South Devon Railway opened as an extension to the South Devon's Tavistock branch. On 21 July 1886 the North Cornwall Railway, a protégé of the LSWR, opened from Halwill, its station being located adjacent to its broad gauge predecessor. The two stations remained independent of each other until 1943 when a connecting line was installed as a wartime measure. After nationalisation, in 1951, the original branch (by then Western Region) station was given the suffix North, and the Southern one was termed South. The former was closed to passengers in 1952, with all trains now handled at the latter. North was, however, retained as a goods depot. Both stations were visited by the Great Western Society's 'Launceston Branch Centenary Tour' on Sunday 5 September 1965. Departing from Exeter St David's at 12.20pm and hauled by No 41283, the tour gained access to the Launceston branch at Lydford

and terminated at the Great Western station. The stock was then shunted into the Southern station and the loco is seen running round at 3.30pm before heading up the North Cornwall line to Halwill, from where it would head the last steam-hauled train to Bude.

The branch closed to passengers in 1962, the goods depot closed in February 1966, and the North Cornwall passenger service ceased in the following October. The exact position of the 'past' photo is within a car dealership, so in a view from a little further forward, we can see that much of the station area is now occupied as a car park by the Launceston Steam Railway. This 1ft 11½in gauge railway runs west from Launceston for 2½ miles through the Kensey Valley over the original North Cornwall formation.
R. A. Lumber/DHM

CAMELFORD: The North Cornwall was extended through Egloskerry to Tresmeer on 21 July 1892 (both stations are now dwellings), with a further extension to Otterham and Camelford opening on 14 August 1893. The new temporary terminus was located at a somewhat remote spot by a crossroads, with the town more than a mile to the south. However, the station was considered to be an important railhead, with Boscastle to the north, Tintagel to the west and Davidstow to the east. Accordingly the main station building (constructed in faced Delabole stone) was provided with an awning over the up platform. These are, however, obscured on 29 August 1960 as 'T9' 4-4-0 No 30709 leaves on the 9.56am Okehampton to Padstow train. It is pictured from a road overbridge.

The signal box and passing loop here remained in use until the end of the passenger service. After closure the bridge was demolished and the road widened, so the same view today is a meaningless one of trees. The station building is occupied as a cycling museum, but the owner did not wish to have the structure photographed when visited in 2006. This affords the opportunity to include a post-closure view taken on 25 June 1967, which shows a long rake of condemned wagons stored on the up road. *Both R. A. Lumber*

DELABOLE: Services were further extended the 2½ miles to this station from 18 October 1893. Again a winding route was taken, on a falling gradient of 1 in 123, and involved a final curve close to the massive slate quarry. Reputedly in continual use since 1555, the quarry provided traffic for the railway, initially mainly in the form of roofing slates, but when clay tiles largely superseded them, markets were found for slate dust. This was once a by-product, but was subsequently ground to powder in a mill; among its uses was the manufacture of 78rpm gramophone records! The station is pictured on a sunny 2 July 1961; the quarry sidings are curving away beyond the main station building, which was located on the down side. Presflo wagons for slate dust can be noted between the buildings at the far end of the down platform.

From 1992 a housing estate has been developed on the site of the station, but the main building still survives as a dwelling, and can be noted to the right of the van in this 30 May 2006 view. The next six 'present' pictures were also taken on this date. *Terry Gough/DHM*

PORT ISAAC ROAD: The section of the North Cornwall Railway from Delabole to Wadebridge opened on 1 June 1895. This isolated station was built on a curve in rolling countryside, more than 3 miles south-east of its namesake village. Port Isaac was a busy fishing port at that time, and no doubt the LSWR was intent on securing some of this business. The line was single track throughout, but each of the stations had crossing loops controlled by signal boxes. None of the intermediate stations between Launceston and Wadebridge had a footbridge, and passengers had to use boarded crossings to change platforms. On 11 April 1956 'N' Class 2-6-0 No 31830 enters the station with a down goods. Half a mile south of here the line passed through Trelill Tunnel, 354 yards long and the only one on the line.

The station is now a private residence. The owners are engaged in car restoration and the goods shed has been adapted as a workshop. *Terry Gough/DHM*

ST KEW HIGHWAY: In an evocative undated scene, station staff return to other duties as an 'N' Class 'Mogul' departs with a three-coach up working. One of these is possibly the porter-signalman heading for his box, which was located just off the platform end, behind the camera. The station was very similar in style and layout to Port Isaac Road, and was adjacent to the main A39 road, with the village of St Kew more than 1½ miles to the north. A small community grew around the station and is still known by this name. The use of 'Highway' rather than 'Road' is intriguing.

This station is also now occupied as a dwelling, and extensive growth in the garden dictated that a different perspective be adopted for the 'present' comparison. The trackbed between the platforms has been filled in, but the coping stones are clearly visible. The down side waiting shelter also survives, but is out of picture. The goods shed (to the left) has been converted into a house, with different occupiers. *E. S. Youldon collection/DHM*

WADEBRIDGE: The town is situated on each side of the ancient Camel river bridge and had a railway from 1834 when the Bodmin & Wadebridge opened. A single-platform station was provided, and this was rebuilt in 1888 when a connection was made with the GWR at Boscarne. With the arrival of the North Cornwall line the station was further enlarged, with the original platform extended and an island platform added. The two railways originally joined at Wadebridge Junction, but from July 1907 the connection was removed and the junction signal box closed. The two routes then entered the town as parallel but separate tracks. In a busy scene from 1 July 1961, ex-GWR 2-6-2T No 4565 is approaching the station with a train from Bodmin Road and is about to pass the station pilot, 2-4-0T No 30586, and 4-6-2 No 34072 *257 Squadron*, which is standing at the island platform with the Padstow portion of the 'Atlantic Coast Express'. Clearly visible between the latter locos is the substantial goods shed.

Shortly afterwards the 'Battle of Britain' 'Pacific' is seen departing past the handsome four-arm upper-quadrant bracket signal, which was controlled by East box (located behind the camera).

Goods service over the North Cornwall line ceased in September 1964 and the route closed completely from 3 October 1966. Passenger services to Padstow and Bodmin ceased from 30 January 1967. However, freight traffic via the latter route ensured the railway's survival here for more than a decade. This included incoming fertiliser and cement loads, while slate dust was brought from Delabole by road for loading in the goods shed. Eventually all this traffic petered out and total closure came on 4 September 1978. However, on the 30th of that month 'The Wadebridge Wanderer' charter operated from Derby, 'Rat' No 25080 hauling the seven coaches from Plymouth. It is pictured before departing with the noon return working; most of the track to the right of this view had been taken out of use in December 1967 when the signal boxes were closed. This was the last loco-hauled train to Wadebridge, but on 17 December the Bodmin Lions Club operated two DMU 'Santa Specials' over the line.

The goods shed survives today, occupied by a pre-school playgroup and youth club. *Terry Gough(2)/DHM(2)*

WADEBRIDGE: 'O2' Class 0-4-4T No 30200 waits with a train for Bodmin North on 12 June 1958; its crew are sitting on the platform seat, enjoying a break in the sunshine. The concrete footbridge was erected in the 1920s when it replaced the original Victorian wooden structure. Clearly visible on the right is the two-road engine shed, which was built of timber on a steel frame in 1895, on spare land near the River Camel. The two roads converged at the west end directly on to a 50-foot turntable. The shed replaced an earlier Bodmin & Wadebridge structure, but was itself extended in 1907 to house the steam railcars that had been introduced on local services. Coded 72F in BR days, the allocation would have been two 'O2s' and the three Beatties at this time. The depot maintained 13 sets of enginemen, divided into several links, the most senior of which covered the Wenford job.

The shed closed to steam on 2 January 1965 and the building was demolished in 1969. Today housing covers much of the railway site with a road following the course of the main running lines. *P. K. Tunks/DHM*

WADEBRIDGE: 'N' Class 2-6-0 No 31834 pauses in the down platform with a Padstow train on 3 July 1961. Note the brazier next to the water column; even mild Cornwall can experience freezing temperatures! Visible on the left is station pilot No 30586, the only one of Wadebridge's famous trio of Joseph Beattie's well tanks to have square splashers, and also the engine only normally used on the Wenford branch when the others were unavailable. This was due to its higher tank filler cap – it took longer to replenish its tanks at the Penhargard water stop. Beyond it is the hoist that stood at the eastern end of the shed. With its parent depot Exmouth Junction 90 miles away, the shed staff needed to be self-sufficient in repair work.

The main station building survives today as the 'John Betjeman Centre' for the aged; the former Poet Laureate had a great love for the area and the North Cornwall Railway is commemorated in his work. *Terry Gough/DHM*

LITTLE PETHERICK CREEK: The Bodmin & Wadebridge Railway started at Wadebridge Quay, to the west of the station, and for many years this was the main outlet for Wenford's china clay and granite traffic. It was not until 27 March 1899, almost four years after reaching Wadebridge, that the North Cornwall was extended beyond this point, and the final leg to Padstow opened. This 5½-mile extension ran along the southern shore of the ever-widening Camel estuary and provided a series of fine vistas for the traveller. The main engineering feature on this section was the viaduct over the wide inlet of Little Petherick, less than a mile from journey's end. An embankment took the rails halfway across the creek, with three 130-foot-long spans, supported on four braced columns, completing the crossing. On Saturday 1 July 1961 SECR-designed 'N' Class 2-6-0 No 31837 is initially seen emerging from a deep cutting through the side of Dennis Hill as it approaches the viaduct with the 6.00pm Padstow to Okehampton train. Moments later, Terry Gough has panned his camera to the right to capture the 'Mogul' and its three coaches as they cross the 20-chain-radius curving structure. An obelisk commemorating Queen Victoria's Jubilee of 1897 surmounts Dennis Hill to the left.

Today this wonderful stretch of former railway is part of the 'Camel Trail' and is enjoyed by thousands of walkers and cyclists each year. Study of the tide times allowed the taking of the 'present' view on a lovely day in May 2006. *Terry Gough (2)/DHM*

PADSTOW: Located on a sheltered inlet from the Camel, which provides a natural anchorage, the port dates from the 16th century with a history of trade with Bristol, Wales and Ireland. Shipbuilding was the dominant industry in the 19th century, but this ended with steam vessels supplanting the traditional wooden sailing boats that were constructed here. The belated arrival of the railway ended years of economic decline and boosted the fishing and tourist industries. Former GWR 2-6-2T No 5553 is pictured departing with the 8.04pm to Bodmin Road on 3 July 1961. It is passing the signal box, with the goods shed in the left foreground. The 70-foot turntable is just out of view on the right; this replaced a 55-foot model in April 1947 and could accommodate the new Bulleid 'Pacifics'. The two sidings on the right lead on to the South Jetty.

It is not possible to use the same vantage point today, but the 17 September 2005 view shows that much of this site is used for car parking. The main station building survives and is used as offices by HM Customs & Excise and the local Town Council. *Terry Gough/DHM*

PADSTOW: 'West Country' 4-6-2 No 34033 *Chard* has arrived with the 7.30am from Waterloo on 1 July 1961, the train completing a journey of almost 260 miles to this farthest-flung outpost on the Southern's system. The building on the left is the Fish Shed, where train-loads of fish were once loaded. However, by this time the industry was in decline and landings were probably being taken away by road. Behind the camera stands the Hotel Metropole; built by the LSWR and opened in 1901 as the South Western Hotel, it successfully catered for its intended market of 'high class' visitors.

Much of the platform survives today, as do the rail posts used for railings, but in recent years a large building containing shop units has been built beside it. *Terry Gough/DHM*

Bodmin & Wadebridge Railway

POLBROCK: The B&WR was one of the oldest railways in the world, a pioneering venture that could claim a number of 'firsts' in Cornwall: the first to be built to standard gauge, the first to use steam locos and the first to carry passengers. Promoted by local landowner Sir William Molesworth of Pencarrow, the object of the railway was to convey limey sea sand from the Camel estuary to treat the acidic soil of inland farms. Although the main line was considered to be the almost 12-mile run from Wadebridge to Wenfordbridge, the section between the former and Bodmin was opened first on 4 July 1834; the Ruthern Bridge branch and Wenford line came into use on 6 August and 30 September respectively. Just over 2 miles from Wadebridge the line passed under a minor road bridge at Polbrock, and No 25080 is seen here with the returning 'Wadebridge Wanderer' tour on 30 September 1978, the loco bearing a wreath.

The bridge survives today, but the view therefrom is a canopy of trees, so a lower angle was selected 27 years later to show the 'Camel Trail' following the formation. *Both DHM*

GROGLEY HALT: In an 1888 improvement to avoid a sharp curve, a deviation was made to the original route about a quarter of a mile before this halt, but the original alignment was retained as a headshunt to gain access to the Ruthern Bridge branch. The latter ran behind the halt, crossed the Camel via a two-span bridge and ran to the south for more than a mile. Inward traffic included sand and coal, with minerals (iron, lead and copper) carried out. Agricultural traffic was mainly carried after the mines closed, and the last train ran in 1933. The timber halt, complete with a GWR 'pagoda roof' shelter, served local farms and settlements beneath Great Grogley Down. It was originally unlit and no trains were allowed to stop after dark. Due to its deteriorating condition it was replaced by the pictured concrete structure in 1957.

The platform survives today; access from the lane on the left is gained via the branch alignment, including the surviving river bridge. *E. S. Youldon collection/DHM*

NANSTALLON HALT: The LSWR assumed control of the B&WR in 1846, in a tactical move designed to keep the broad gauge interests out of north Cornwall, but it was to be almost 50 years before the line connected with the rest of its system. The halts at Grogley, Nanstallon and Dunmere all opened on 2 July 1906, a month after a steam railmotor service was introduced on the route. The latter halts were also provided with 'pagoda' shelters, and these survived until the end of passenger services. Also visible is the small signal box, which was not a block post but controlled the level crossing over a minor road. The distant signal is for Boscarne Junction, less than half a mile to the east. Beyond the crossing is a siding that closed to traffic in 1960.

This platform is also still in situ beside the 'Camel Trail'. *E .S. Youldon collection/DHM*

BOSCARNE JUNCTION was the end of more than 4½ miles of Electric Tablet-controlled single line from Wadebridge East, the signal box also controlling the level crossing. The B&WR's isolation from the main railway network ended on 3 September 1888, but the connection was not with its parent the LSWR. Instead the GWR opened an extension of its Bodmin branch to Boscarne with running powers through to Wadebridge.

The second view is from the location's final days as part of the national system. No 37186 has arrived with BR's 'Cornish Branch Lines Railtour' of Saturday 19 November 1983. No 37187 is at the far end of the seven-coach 1Z10 0815 from Bristol Temple Meads, which had earlier visited Carne Point and Parkandillick. This was the final locomotive-hauled train to this spot before the preservation era, while a BR-organised DMU excursion from St Austell on the following day was to be the last train. After closure to Wadebridge, some track was left in situ for a short distance beyond the crossing as a headshunt. *Author's collection/DHM*

BOSCARNE JUNCTION: In May 1964 two platforms were constructed at a cost of £2,000 in the 'vee' of the junction, with a rail-level platform provided on the Bodmin North line, and a normal-height one on the Bodmin General route. Boscarne Exchange Platform opened on 15 June, from which date an AC railbus provided a shuttle between there and Bodmin North, connecting with the single-unit railcar operating the Bodmin Road to Padstow service. The oil-lit timber platforms were only accessible by rail. In the 'past' photograph, taken from the signal box, a Bodmin Road-bound 'bubble car' single unit is heading for a connection with No W79977, which can be glimpsed on the left. Withdrawal of all passenger services in the area took place on 30 January 1967.

On 3 September 2005 ex-GWR 2-6-2T No 5552 has arrived with the 1320 from General. The 'Camel Trail' passes the site on the left. *Author's collection/DHM*

BOSCARNE JUNCTION: On Monday 3 July 1961 well tank No 30585 arrives with the daily return working from Wenfordbridge. The hut contains a ground frame that controlled the connections at the east end of the yard. The site had four lines, the one in the foreground (the south side of the layout) leading to the Western's Bodmin General. Next to it is the No 1 interchange siding, into which traffic from the Southern was shunted to await collection by a Western train. Goods traffic from the WR was left in the northern siding (No 2) on the left, with Bodmin North and Wenford trains running between the two sidings.

The 'present' view includes the platform erected by the Bodmin & Wenford Railway on the site of the former Bodmin North running line in 1996, services from Bodmin General commencing in August of that year. *Terry Gough/DHM*

DUNMERE JUNCTION: After leaving Boscarne, the line ran for about 10 chains before reaching this junction, crossing the Camel en route. When originally built, the line had crossed the river a little to the south, with the Bodmin route leaving the Wenford line further to the north, before then crossing the main Bodmin to Wadebridge road. Improvements made during the 1896-91 period provided a new course for the Bodmin branch for some three-quarters of a mile to eliminate the level crossing and to ease the steep gradients. On 19 September 1964 0-6-0PT No 1369 is heading for Wenfordbridge with the 'Wenford Special' brake-van tour. The shed housed a permanent way trolley, and the Bodmin North route in the foreground is at a noticeably higher level. The junction was operated by the Wenford train guard from a ground frame housed in a hut to the left of this view. Once the train was on the branch he would have to walk back to Boscarne Junction box with the single-line tablet before returning to his train.

Both routes are now part of the 'Camel Trail'. The shed just about survives, and the original B&WR gate posts can be noted on the left. *Peter W. Gray/DHM*

DUNMERE HALT: The later alignment to Bodmin followed a right-hand curve at a rising gradient of 1 in 40 for a short distance before reaching this halt. The platform was constructed adjacent to an overbridge that carried the Bodmin to Wadebridge road, a path running down from the road; concrete posts marking its course can be noted in this undated view taken from beneath the bridge. Dunmere level crossing is a short distance down this road, to the right. None of the three 1906 halts was staffed, and tickets were issued and collected by the train guard. The line continued to climb from here at gradients averaging 1 in 47.

The 'Camel Trail' follows the formation behind the camera towards the outskirts of Bodmin. Access to a large car park for trail users is obtained via a path immediately to the left – note the wooden railings in the 2005 picture. *E. S. Youldon collection/DHM*

BODMIN NORTH: Just outside the terminus the railway passed Bodmin Gaol, and in its early years excursions were run for those wishing to witness public executions! While the aforementioned improvements to the alignment were being made, a new station was built here, the passenger service ceasing from 1 November 1886 for no fewer than nine years. The suffix 'North' was added to the name in 1949 after nationalisation. Former LSWR 'O2' Class 0-4-4T No 30200 waits to leave from the single-platform station with the 2pm departure to Padstow on 10 September 1960. The Adams tanks had dominated this service since early in the century.

Although the background houses remain to help identify this location today, the station has been erased from the landscape, with a road following the formation and a car park and commercial activity on the site. Rather than repeat the uninspiring view seen in No 17 of this series, a scene from behind the buffers features 0-6-0PT No 4694. This loco and No 4666 took over the service in 1960, although as seen above No 30200 was retained as spare engine. Ivatt 2-6-2Ts then assumed control in 1962. *Peter W. Gray/E. S. Youldon collection*

DUNMERE CROSSING: Beattie 2-4-0WT No 30585 passes over the ungated A389 crossing on 3 July 1961 with the daily freight to Wenfordbridge. It will shortly pass a siding known as Dunmere Wharf, mainly used for grain to a nearby mill. Originally built by Beyer Peacock in 1874-75 for London suburban duties, the first well tank arrived at Wadebridge by sea in 1893. After the LSWR finally connected with the B&WR, three rebuilt examples were allocated to Wadebridge, as, owing to their short wheelbase and light construction, they were found to be eminently suited for working the Wenford and Ruthern Bridge lines. Other loco types were subsequently tried or considered for these duties, but none was deemed appropriate, and the tanks reigned supreme for an incredible 69 years. One was usually spare each day with the others undertaking the Wenford branch and the Wadebridge pilot jobs. Their longevity ensured that the line was regularly visited in later years by enthusiasts paying homage to these remarkable machines, two of which have since entered preservation.

The siding was removed in 1969, but rails are still embedded in the road surface today. *Terry Gough/DHM*

PENHARGARD: Beyond Dunmere crossing the B&WR line followed the course of the Camel on a steep embankment with sharp curves abounding on the sinuous route. Over a mile from Dunmere, another siding was located at Penhargard until about 1925, mainly for loading timber. A little further on a water tank was provided in Pencarrow Woods, as neither the well tanks, nor their successors from the ex-GWR '1366' Class, had sufficient water capacity without replenishing their tanks in both directions. Indeed, if there was a lot of shunting activity at Wenford the loco sometimes needed to make a quick trip back to the tank for a 'top-up'. The tank was fed by gravity from a passing stream. Replacements for the 2-4-0Ts arrived in August 1962 in the form of three 0-6-0PTs recently made redundant by diesel shunters from their duties on Weymouth Quay. On 27 April 1963 No 1369 is seen taking water while working the RCTS/PRC 'Camel Valleyman' brake-van railtour.

Rather than include a view of the tree-lined trail (which can be seen in the original Cornwall volume in this series), No 1369 is seen again departing with the Plymouth Railway Circle's 'Wenford Special' of 19 September 1964. *Both R. A. Lumber*

HELLANDBRIDGE: The track emerged from the trees as it approached Helland Wharf siding, used mainly for feedstuffs and closed in 1960. Shortly afterwards the line passed between two cottages before passing over a minor road by way of another ungated crossing. The travelling shunter is walking towards the crossing on 28 September 1978 before supervising the safe passage of No 08377 and its load of china clay from Wenford. The line was dieselised towards the end of 1964, with Class 03 204hp diesel shunters employed. However, these were both under-powered and unreliable, and were replaced within a couple of years by engines from the excellent 350hp Class 08.

A visit in September 2005 revealed that rails remain embedded in the tarmac at the site of this crossing. *Both DHM*

WENFORD: The Wenford line was always freight-only and for many years the bulk of the traffic, and in later times all of it, originated at the china clay works located here. The clay was mined on Stannon Moor, about 6 miles to the north-east, from where it was piped in slurry form to the works for drying and loading into timber-sided rail wagons. In early years it was exported via the wharves at Padstow and Wadebridge, but after the GWR reached Boscarne most loads were left there to be taken out via that route to the docks at Fowey. On 3 July 1961 No 30585 has just arrived with a train of empties; bagged clay will be loaded into the covered vans.

In later years traffic levels were erratic, and gradually reduced in volume. There was a need to replace the ageing wagon fleet and invest in the track, but such expenditure was not considered to be justified and the final train ran on 26 September 1983. The works remained open, with clay taken away by road, and after the Bodmin & Wenford Railway commenced operations, attempts were made to reinstate this stretch of line. Unfortunately local opposition stymied this, mainly due to the 'Camel Trail' having taken over the trackbed. In any event, the works closed in about 2002, and was put up for sale in 2005. In recent years the clay companies have faced fierce competition from abroad, and mining at Stannon has ceased. The trail originally ended at Poley's Bridge, just across the road from the works, but in 2006 an extension to Wenfordbridge was opened. It runs along the edge of the site, to the right of the 'present' view. *Terry Gough/DHM*

WENFORDBRIDGE: The B&WR continued for more than a quarter of a mile to its terminus, where at one time a siding continued over a road and curved right to connect with a tramway owned by De Lank Quarry. This standard gauge line ran up the hillside by means of a cable-worked 1 in 8 incline to a granite quarry, and much of the stone used in constructing London's bridges emanated from here. Trains of granite were despatched regularly from the late 19th century until traffic ceased in the 1940s. The Southern Railway provided a 5-ton overhead crane here, mainly for loading timber, and this is just in view on 3 July 1961 as No 30585 shunts a coal wagon. Coal for domestic use was the major inward traffic.

The goods depot closed in 1967 with the track from here to just north of the clay works lifted during 1971. The site was then used for more than 20 years as a coal yard, but as previously mentioned the 'Camel Trail' was extended here in January 2006, and picnic tables and a car park can be seen today. *Terry Gough/DHM*

Callington branch

CALSTOCK: The 3ft 6in gauge East Cornwall Mineral Railway opened from Calstock to Kelly Bray in 1872. This 7½-mile line was built to serve the mining interests around Gunnislake, Stoke Climsland and Kelly Bray, and the quarries on Kit Hill. Calstock is situated on the steep sides of the Tamar Valley and was a busy port with sailing barges bringing in coal and taking out the tin, copper and arsenic produced by the mines. A 35-chain cable-worked 1 in 6 incline operated between Calstock Quay and the railway on the hillside above. Two steam locos were used on the upper section, with horses employed on the quay. Following the success of the line, there were various proposals to connect with the main railway system. Eventually the Plymouth, Devonport & South Western Junction Railway, which had opened its line from Lydford to Devonport in 1890, acquired the ECMR and rebuilt it, connecting with its line at Bere Alston. To carry the rails 120 feet above the Tamar, a 12-arch viaduct was constructed of concrete blocks; each arch is of 60-foot span. To replace the incline a wagon lift was erected adjacent to the second arch to provide access to the quay, but this was removed in September 1934. On 15 April 1961 'O2' 0-4-4T No 30225 is seen crossing this graceful structure with the 4.23pm from Callington.

The viaduct remains today as a wonderful addition to the scenic splendour of the valley. All of the 'present' pictures on this branch were taken on 29 June 2006. *Peter W. Gray/DHM*

GUNNISLAKE: From Calstock the branch runs high above the Tamar in a south-easterly direction before turning through 180 degrees, then heading north to this station. The town is a little to the north and the station was built adjacent to the village of Drakewalls, which had been the name of the ECMR's depot on the same spot. This was the only passing point on the new line and had an island platform accessed by a short subway under the down road. Ivatt 2-6-2T No 41316 is arriving with the 6.01pm Bere Alston to Gunnislake train on 4 July 1961. This was actually a through working from Plymouth, but not mentioned as such in the public timetable.

The branch is still open to here as it continues to serve a geographically remote area that has poor road access to Plymouth. However, there was a low road bridge over the A390 immediately to the south of the station, and to allow its demolition a new re-sited station was opened on 6 June 1994. The 2006 view shows this road in the foreground, and the 'new' platform is located next to the fencing visible to the left of the nearest car. A housing estate has been developed on the station site behind the camera. *Terry Gough/DHM*

CHILSWORTHY: The new branch opened to both passengers and freight on 2 March 1908, but this halt, less than a mile from Gunnislake, did not open until June 1909. The single platform was located on the north side of the line, high on a hillside with a magnificent view across the Tamar Valley. At different times there were several sidings in the immediate vicinity serving a mine, quarries and a brick & tile works. On 15 April 1961 'O2' No 30225 is pictured after leaving with the 5.23pm train from Bere Alston to Callington. The halt can be glimpsed adjacent to the overbridge in the left distance.

Finding this spot in 2006 required a little legwork. The metal footbridge seen just behind the train survives today, carrying a public footpath. However, the cutting beneath it is filled with dense undergrowth. Other tree growth meant that the comparison view had to be taken a little further forward and to the right of the original. The house is the same one visible on the right of the 'past' scene and the line of trees to the left marks the track formation. The platform survives, but the trackbed next to it is very overgrown – even more so than in the view in the original Cornwall volume. *Peter W. Gray/DHM*

LATCHLEY: From Chilsworthy the line continued to climb, with one section as steep as 1 in 44, for just over a mile before reaching this halt. Named after a village more than a mile to the north and some 500 feet lower, it was opened with the branch at the site of the ECMR's Cox's Park depot. 'O2' Class 0-4-4T No 30225 is crossing a minor road as it runs into the halt with the 4.23pm from Callington on 15 April 1961. The ungated crossing has no fewer than three warning signs on the approach: 'L&SWR Beware of Trains', 'Crossing No Gates' and 'Trains Cross Here' – today's Health & Safety Executive would be proud of them! 'O2s' took over the passenger duties on this line in 1929, but would be totally replaced by Ivatt tanks in 1961.

The gate posts on the left (leading to a house) survive to mark the spot today. Also, just visible on the right is the original Mineral Railway's station house, and the platform is still in situ within its grounds. *Peter W. Gray/DHM*

CALLINGTON: The terminus of the 9½-mile branch was actually in Kelly Bray, about a mile north of Callington, and the ECMR depot had been named accordingly. For a short period after opening the station was more accurately designated as Callington Road. It had an overall roof, which can be seen on 2 July 1961 as 2-6-2T No 41302 waits with the 1.00pm departure to Bere Alston. Formerly this roof extended across the adjoining track to form a carriage shed. The run-round loop was to the right and it was necessary for an arriving train to reverse out of the platform to perform this manoeuvre. A two-road wooden engine shed was next to the loop; it normally housed two engines, sub-shedded from Plymouth (Friary).

The last train on the branch from here to Gunnislake ran on 5 November 1966, and today the station site is occupied both commercially and residentially. The houses on Station Road link the two pictures. *Terry Gough/DHM*

Saltash to Par (the Cornwall Railway)

SALTASH: The River Tamar provides a natural boundary for much of the border between Devon and Cornwall, and the major engineering work required during construction of the Cornwall Railway was the Royal Albert Bridge, built to carry the route from the Duchy to Plymouth on the far shore. At this point the river is 1,100 feet wide with a maximum depth of 80 feet. Additionally the Admiralty insisted that there was a clear headway of 100 feet at high water to give clearance for naval vessels. This structure is one of Isambard Kingdom Brunel's greatest achievements, and one that has provided a lasting tribute to the abilities of that outstanding engineer. Pictured from Saltash station's down platform, No 6845 *Paviland Grange* crosses with the 1.15pm Tavistock Junction to Penzance goods on Saturday 9 January 1960.

The ladders and walkways giving access to the tubes normally used to partially obscure the lettering on the end towers, but they were removed in 2006 as part of the Brunel bicentennial celebrations. A Penzance to Paddington HST crosses on 29 May 2006. *Derek Frost/DHM*

SALTASH station is built on a curve immediately west of the Royal Albert Bridge. On 29 April 1971 Class 42 'Warship' No 868 *Zephyr* is pictured from the adjacent road bridge as it starts to cross with the 6M11 1450 St Erth to Kensington milk train. The original wrought-iron approach spans were replaced by steel ones in about 1928. The Victorian Baptist church is prominent beyond the station.

The 0830 Penzance to Dundee Virgin Voyager service is seen crossing at the maximum allowed speed of 15mph. The adjacent 1961 road bridge generates a fair amount of turbulence and is a hazard to workers on the rail bridge. This and the next four 'present' pictures were taken on a windy 29 May 2006, and holding the camera steady was something of a problem! The church was destroyed by fire on Christmas Day 1987, but its replacement can be noted. *John Medley/DHM*

SALTASH: Collett-designed 4-6-0 No 7820 *Dinmore Manor* passes through the station with what is thought to be the 12.40pm Doublebois to Tavistock Junction Class 'K' local goods on 9 January 1960. To its right is the well-stocked Wyman's kiosk; once a well-known feature of stations on this line; the company won the Great Western contract for station bookstalls from W. H. Smith in 1905.

In 2006 No 158871 pauses with the 0747 Penzance to Portsmouth Harbour service. The main station building is still standing, but boarded up. There are plans to develop it as the 'Brunel Heritage Centre', with this structure retained to provide a gallery and exhibition space. An extension will include a café and shop, with a viewing area that will overlook the Royal Albert Bridge. *Derek Frost/DHM*

SALTASH: A pair of North British Type 2 diesel-hydraulics approach with a Penzance train on 9 July 1960. The signal box can be noted beyond the covered station footbridge in the foreground. Work is under way on the new road bridge, which was to open for traffic in October 1961; until then a ferry service was provided for road transport. However, the railway had offered easy access to and from Plymouth and substantial numbers of commuters and shoppers were carried before the bridge opened. Steam railmotors were used on an intensive service between Saltash and Plympton from 1904, and new halts were opened in the Plymouth district. Auto-trains later augmented the steam motors and by the early 1930s this suburban service amounted to almost 50 trains each weekday.

The same viewpoint today is largely obscured by trees, so a position on the adjacent road overbridge was selected to record No 158855 arriving forming a Gloucester to Penzance service. The station has been unstaffed since 1971 and the footbridge has been demolished, passengers now also using the road bridge. *Hugh Davies/DHM*

47

SALTASH: Looking in the opposite direction from the same bridge, Class 52 No D1050 *Western Ruler* is approaching with the 1A43 0915 Penzance to Paddington train in October 1969. The train is hiding a short loop siding, with the two-track goods yard away to the right, where milk tanks are being loaded. The train has just crossed the curving 203-yard-long Coombe-by-Saltash Viaduct, a masonry structure that replaced a timber viaduct in 1894. Beyond the viaduct the line runs along the hillside above the Tamar in a southerly direction, compared with its westerly crossing of the Royal Albert Bridge.

Track in the goods yard was removed in 1972 and housing with car parking now occupies the site, while the signal box and semaphores ceased to be in use after 2 July 1973. Nos 43128 and 43146 are powering the 0904 Penzance to Paddington HST. *Bernard Mills/DHM*

DEFIANCE PLATFORM: Less than a mile from Saltash station, this single-platform halt opened in 1905, constructed above Wearde Quay by the men of HMS *Defiance*, a nearby Torpedo Training School. However, within a year the track was doubled from Saltash to Wearde, on a new alignment, and a new station was built. Although this closed on 27 October 1930, the remains of the platforms are still visible at 3.48pm on 25 July 1959 as Nos 6826 *Nannerth Grange* and 6931 *Aldborough Hall* double-head the 9.30am Paddington to Newquay train. Note the Royal Navy vessel on the right. The down goods loop was created in 1943 by extending a refuge siding, and follows the alignment of the original single-track main line.

Power cars Nos 43126 and 43009 pass the overgrown site with the 0730 Paddington to Penzance HST. These photos were taken from a road bridge leading down to Wearde Quay. *Peter W. Gray/DHM*

WEARDE: Looking in the opposite direction from the previous photos, No 6815 *Frilford Grange* is passing the signal box with the 7.30am Penzance to Bristol train on 25 July 1959 – the down goods loop is running in on the left. A water column is available for locos waiting in the loop, and a water tower can be noted opposite the box. In 1908 a double-track deviation, almost 4 miles long, was opened from here to St Germans. The original single-track alignment had included five timber viaducts, but the new route followed an inland course with easier gradients, reduced track curvature and only three viaducts. The carriage sidings seen running to the left of the fourth coach in the photo are on the original formation.

The carriage sidings were taken out of use and the signal box closed in October 1963. The goods loop was truncated at the same time and now formed a refuge siding, accessed at the Saltash end. On 28 June 2003 No 66046 passes with the 6Z05 0900 Carne Point to Tavistock Junction china clay empties, which will be loaded at Marsh Mills on the remaining stub of the Launceston branch. *Peter W. Gray/DHM*

WEARDE: In a photo of inferior quality but nonetheless full of interest, we can see Wearde box in the foreground, with the hulk of HMS *Defiance* to the right. This was the ninth ship so named when launched at Pembroke Dock in 1861. However, it was immediately obsolete with the introduction of ironclad ships, and placed into the reserve fleet. In 1884 it was commissioned as the new Torpedo School ship and moored in the Hamoaze off Wearde Quay, a tidal area by the entrance to the River Lynher. The training involved firing live submarine mines and torpedoes on the river! In a somewhat complex story, other vessels were added to or displaced from the school and by about 1922 it comprised the original *Defiance*, the cruiser HMS *Spartan*, the corvette *Cleopatra* and an accommodation hulk previously named *Inconstant*; the latter ships were renamed *Defiance II*, *III* and *IV* respectively. It is this period that is believed to be recorded in the picture. The original Defiance was withdrawn in 1930 and replaced, and the school closed in 1954 and moved to Portsmouth. *Lens of Sutton Association*

In another complementary photo, D1039 *Western King* approaches Coombe-by-Saltash Viaduct with a Ponsandane to Exeter Riverside freight on 29 April 1971. The bridge from which the photos on pages 49 and 50 were taken is in the background, and the truncated goods loop is on the left; it was taken out of use in the following year. *John Medley*

FORDER VIADUCT: When the 53-mile-long Cornwall Railway opened from Plymouth to Truro in April 1859 there were 34 viaducts in addition to the Royal Albert Bridge, with an aggregate length of approximately 4 miles. On no other main-line railway in the UK were there so many viaducts per mile. Financial constraints and geography combined to test Brunel's skill in the design of cheap but effective structures to carry the broad gauge across the many tidal inlets and deep river valleys that intersected the route. On this railway, for inland viaducts he introduced a combination of masonry piers carrying a simple timber superstructure. Only where the line crossed a tidal creek was there a need to employ timber piles in the interests of economy, and thus an all-timber construction was used. Despite the limitations of timber as a structural material, some of these viaducts lasted into the 20th century, and in a tribute to Brunel's original designs there was never an accident with one. The original 202-yard-long timber Forder Viaduct crossed Forder Lake, an inlet of the Lynher River. The 1908 deviation to the north, at the head of Antony Passage, included a 234-yard-long masonry structure, 69 feet above the high water mark. Laira's '2884' Class 2-8-0 No 3862 crosses with a down goods at 12.40pm on 18 April 1960. The Plymouth depot normally only had one or two of these locos allocated, and with none based in Cornwall they were relatively rare performers in the Duchy.

Steam could be seen again in this delightful setting on 9 May 1998 when 4-6-0 No 6024 *King Edward I* headed the 1Z56 0640 Coventry to Par 'The Par King Pioneer' charter. This class was barred from the Duchy in steam days, but are now permitted following strengthening of the Royal Albert Bridge. *Peter W. Gray/DHM*

53

ST GERMANS: This original Cornwall Railway station was built on a reverse curve with the main building on the up side. In this undated view the signal box can be noted at the far end of the down platform; the goods yard is out of sight around the curve to the left. The 1908 deviation ended just east of the station after crossing a viaduct over the River Tiddy. This 13-arch structure was the longest and highest of the three new viaducts, and is 326 yards long and 99 feet above high water. The line to the west of the station was doubled in 1895.

The goods yard closed in 1965, but the signal box lasted until May 1973. A panel was then operational in a room at the east end of the down platform building, acting as an interface between the Plymouth panel and Liskeard signal box, but this ended in April 1998. The building on the up side is now a dwelling offering bed and breakfast facilities, and is about to be passed by an HST on 29 May 2006. Converted ex-GWR clerestory roofed TPO No 841 of 1889 stands in the former up-side goods dock, providing accommodation for six persons, and former LSWR Luggage Van No 1353 performs a similar function at the other end of the station. *Lens Of Sutton Association/ DHM(2)*

COLDRENICK VIADUCT: Just to the east of Menheniot station the railway crosses the valley of the River Seaton by means of a curving viaduct 265 yards long and 138 feet high. In 1895 work started to replace the wooden superstructure, with the original 12 masonry piers raised in brick to take latticed steel girders. Sadly, while a work gang was engaged in fixing one of the new girders in February 1897 a temporary platform collapsed and 12 men fell to their deaths. In 1933 the piers were encased in granite to provide a more substantial support; this was probably considered necessary due to the curvature of the structure. After a gap of more than 21 years, steam returned to the Cornish main line on 6 September 1985 as part of the 'GW150' celebrations. No 7029 *Clun Castle* is pictured working a 1510 Truro to Plymouth excursion.

More prosaic is the use of a Class 150/2 forming the 1119 Penzance to Plymouth service on 29 May 2006. *Both DHM*

LISKEARD: Prairie tank No 4569 is coming off the access line to the Looe branch on 21 June 1956 and is about to cross to the down main. The signal box dates from 1915 when it replaced an earlier box on the up platform. Beyond it are the down refuge sidings, on land that until 1918 had been occupied by a small engine shed. Just to the east of this area is the 240-yard-long Liskeard Viaduct, which carries the main line across the Liskeard Valley (and the Looe branch). Two more sidings are just visible behind the loco, and to the left of the water tower a footpath leads to the branch platform.

The signal box still controls one of the remaining pockets of semaphore signalling in Cornwall, but the connection with the down main was replaced by a new arrangement that gave direct access to the branch for trains of empty clay wagons from the west. Freightliner's No 66530 eases off the branch with the 6M37 1530 Moorswater to Earles Sidings cement empties on 29 June 2006. The loco will run round its train in the station. *Hugh Davies/DHM*

LISKEARD: No 6945 *Glasfryn Hall* runs in with the 3.40pm Plymouth to Penzance train on 8 July 1958. 4-6-0s with smaller driving wheels such as the 'Hall' and 'Grange' classes were well suited to the hilly Cornish main line, and both types were allowed to work 11 coaches (385 tons) unaided between Plymouth and Penzance. The former were also the mainstay of goods trains. No 6945 was then based at Laira but was soon to move on to Westbury. Almost all services within Cornwall were operated by Plymouth or Duchy-based engines, and it was rare for a Cornish locomotive to work east of Newton Abbot.

As seen above, a large building existed on the down platform, but this has since been demolished with only a simple waiting shelter now provided. Track Machine No DR 73920 passes through on 29 May 2006. *Terry Gough/DHM*

LISKEARD: It was decided in the early days of modernisation planning that the West of England would be one of the first areas to abandon steam, and as part of this process Laira began receiving North British Type 2 diesel-hydraulics in March 1959. By the date of this photo more than 30 of this type were based there and had taken over many Cornish workings. Nos D6329 and D6323 are arriving with the 1200 Penzance to Manchester train on Tuesday 16 August 1960; the leading loco had only been delivered two months previously, and steam operation on the Western in Cornwall largely ceased in 1962. As Liskeard station was built in a cutting, the main building (which included the booking hall and station master's office) was located above the platforms at road level, and can be glimpsed in the top right of the photo.

This building was renovated in a $835,000 scheme during 2004-05. 'Sprinter' No 158855 arrives forming the 1319 Penzance to Paignton service on 29 May 2006. *Derek Frost/DHM*

LISKEARD: At the west end of the station a goods shed and yard were built on levelled land. Due to the need to access this yard, the down platform extended further westward than the up one. Two sidings served the wooden shed, with a third leading to a dock, and an up refuge siding was adjacent to the main line. The latter falls away at a gradient of 1 in 59 towards Moorswater Viaduct. The Liskeard to Looe road crosses over the station by means of the bridge seen in the previous pictures, and in this view therefrom Type 2 (by now Class 22) No 6323 is seen again on 23 November 1970 as it stands in the yard with an up freight. The buses are parked in the yard approach road.

Closure of the yard and removal of the track in 1981 allowed for an extension to be added to the up platform. 'Skips' Nos 67011 and 67026 approach with the 6C06 1126 St Blazey to Tavistock Junction clay empties on 17 September 2002. St Blazey depot was still servicing locos used on Royal Mail trains at this time, and rather than send these locos to Plymouth light engine they were used on this working. *Bernard Mills/DHM*

MOORSWATER VIADUCT: The original crossing of the wide, open valley of the East Looe River was made on a curving lofty structure comprising 12 imposing fully buttressed piers, together with a masonry plinth built into the embankment at each end, and with a timber superstructure. However, there seems to have been some concerns regarding the strength and stability of the viaduct, possibly due to the collapse of two of the piers during construction. In any event the original structure saw service for only 22 years before being replaced by a new masonry viaduct just to the north. Comprising eight arches, each of 80-foot span, it is 268 yards long and opened in 1881. There are sharp curves on the approaches to the viaduct at both ends, and the one at the western end is seen from a footbridge at 2.44pm on 4 July 1959 as No 1006 *County of Cornwall* attacks the climb of almost 3 miles to the summit of the route at Doublebois with the 8.25am Paddington to Penzance train.

The viaduct is just visible as the 1005 Paddington to Penzance HST (Nos 43171 and 43139) accelerates by on 29 June 2006. Some almost complete piers of the original structure remain today (see page 83). *Peter W. Gray/DHM*

DOUBLEBOIS: From the east there is a gradient of 1 in 58 on the final stretch to this station, and westbound unfitted goods trains had to stop here to pin down wagon brakes before descending at an average 1 in 70 to Bodmin Road. Coming the other way on 23 May 1961, No 1006 *County of Cornwall* is seen again, with what is probably the 2.00pm Perishable train from Penzance to Crewe, the load including milk tanks. Traffic to markets in London, the Midlands and the North would be carried in through vans. The loco appropriately spent much of its working life in the Duchy, and at different times was allocated to Laira, Penzance, Truro and St Blazey. The station opened in 1860 to serve both a hamlet of the same name and nearby Dobwalls. An ammunition depot was established here in 1943 and these sidings were later used for track panel assembly.

The station closed in October 1964 and the permanent way yard followed suit in 1968. The site today is unrecognisable, and in a view from the road bridge Nos 43192 and 43125 power the 1205 Paddington to Penzance HST on 29 May 2006. *Peter W. Gray/DHM*

BODMIN ROAD: In the 6 miles from Doublebois the line descends sharply through the densely wooded countryside of the Glynn Valley. For much of the distance the line is high up on the south side of the valley, with the River Fowey below. There are no fewer than eight viaducts on this section and the line was singled across and between St Pinnock (the highest in Cornwall) and Largin Viaducts in 1964 in an economy measure. Largin signal box was opened in an isolated location to the west of the latter in 1906. There was no mains supply here, and water for the signalman was delivered by train; the box closed in 1991. Bodmin Road station was built on a curve in a delightful rural setting. It is seen to advantage at 9.15am on 19 July 1958 as No 6823 *Oakley Grange* starts to climb with the 7.50am Newquay to Manchester train.

Undergrowth in the foreground has obscured much of this view in 2006, so looking back to 6 October 1982 the 1500 Penzance to Paddington HST (Nos 43127 and 43128) is seen leaving. *Peter W. Gray/DHM*

BODMIN ROAD: Despite being Cornwall's county town at the time, Bodmin's location meant that it was bypassed when the Cornwall Railway opened, and the town's residents had to make the journey to this station after it opened for custom on 27 June 1859. The line had opened on 4 May, and initially passengers used a private station at Respryn to the west, which otherwise served Lanhydrock House. After several aborted attempts, a 3½-mile standard gauge branch finally opened on 27 May 1887. The main line was to stay broad gauge for another five years, so the branch remained isolated during this period; the station was rebuilt to accommodate the branch. St Blazey's 1924-vintage 2-6-2T No 4565 waits in the branch platform with a Wadebridge train on 12 June 1958.

A Class 108 DMU forming the Cornwall Railway Society's 'Bodmin Septet' Railtour was pictured on 20 May 1995 prior to departure, while a down HST service can be glimpsed arriving in the background. *P. K. Tunks/DHM*

BODMIN ROAD: Despite its short length, the branch climbed almost 300 feet with gradients as severe as 1 in 37. It was expensive to construct, with many cuttings, embankments and bridges. Prairie tank No 5519 drifts in from Bodmin some time in the early post-war period. The rails running past the water tank lead to the up-side goods yard, where a transfer platform was in use while there was the break in gauge; it was used as a cattle dock in later years.

Pannier tank No 4612 and Prairie tank No 5552 arrive with the 1015 from Bodmin General on 3 September 2005. The three sidings on the left are used by the Bodmin & Wenford Railway for stock storage. Just out of view to the left is an exchange siding with the national network. For a while this was used for commercial freight in the form of light fittings from Bodmin, but ceased when EWS considered the operation to be uneconomic. *Lens of Sutton Association/DHM*

BODMIN ROAD: In a view from the down platform on 10 September 1960, 2-6-2T No 4569 is busy shunting coaching stock. The main line can be seen descending westwards at a gradient of 1 in 65, while the track in the left foreground leads to the wooden goods shed, through which the line ran to serve china clay dries. The signal box here was located on the down platform next to the footbridge.

General goods traffic ceased in 1963, with the clay traffic ending in 1966, and the yard site is now used as a car park. Re-named Bodmin Parkway from 4 November 1983, the station has reverted to its original role since the branch closed. The signal box also closed in 1983 and is now a café. Virgin Trains' 0830 Penzance to Dundee Voyager service (No 221144) approaches on 29 June 2006. A Ruston & Hornsby diesel, No 3 *Lec*, can be noted on the right. *Peter W. Gray/DHM*

LOSTWITHIEL: Pictured from the A390 road bridge, Class 22 No 6318 is towing preserved 0-6-0ST No 1363 over the up goods loop on 1 May 1971, returning it to Bodmin Road from an open day at St Blazey shed. From there the saddle tank worked under its own steam down the branch to the Great Western Society's depot at Bodmin. The up loop was added during the Second World War, while the down loop (on the right) came into use in 1936. The connection in the left foreground is with the milk siding. Prominent on the distant hillside is the Norman Restormel Castle, which enjoys a commanding position overlooking the River Fowey valley. Its circular walls are more than 8 feet thick and 100 yards around, and are believed to date from about 1200.

The goods loops exist today, mainly used for running round clay trains. On 29 May 2006 Standard Class 4MT 2-6-0 No 76079 approaches with the 1645 Plymouth to Carne Point 'Fowey Pony' charter. *John Medley/DHM*

LOSTWITHIEL: Looking in the opposite direction at 1801 on 3 May 1969, Class 52 No D1057 *Western Chieftain* is leaving with the four-coach 1620 Penzance to Plymouth stopper. In the background, sister diesel-hydraulic No D1004 *Western Crusader* is entering the station on the 1710 Plymouth to Penzance train. On the right is the Unigate Milk Depot, which opened in 1932 and was to provide traffic for the railway for nearly 50 years. Six-wheel glass-lined 3,000-gallon milk tankers can be noted on both the milk siding to the right, and a siding off the down loop.

Bulk milk traffic by rail ceased during 1980, and although there is still a small milk depot here, much of the site forms the Restormel Industrial Estate. The inevitable tree growth meant that a more head-on stance had to be adopted to record the 1005 Penzance to Paddington HST (power cars Nos 43037 and 43182) on 29 June 2006. The overgrown milk siding is still in situ. *R. A. Lumber/DHM*

LOSTWITHIEL: Pictured from the cattle dock, Prairie tank No 4585 is busily engaged in shunting milk tankers in about 1959. The milk depot is out of view to the left; the dock had once helped supply a nearby slaughter house. Behind the photographer is a level crossing, and immediately beyond that is the station; the signal box is located between the two. From 1895 to 1923 a second box was positioned on the down side, opposite the goods shed.

The signal box is still open, controlling the station area with a fine array of semaphore signals. Palisade fencing has been erected to prevent access to the dock and it was not possible to obtain a satisfactory picture in 2006. Looking back to 16 September 1994, No 37672 *Freight Transport Association* has run round its Goonbarrow Junction to Carne Point china clay train in the down goods loop, and is waiting for the road. The numbers on top of the posts next to the up main indicate to the drivers of seven-, eight- or nine-coach trains where to stop. *Keith Batchelor collection/DHM*

LOSTWITHIEL: The passenger service to Fowey did not commence until 1895, and a bay platform was provided for this on the east side of the station. On 14 April 1956 St Blazey's auto-fitted '1400' Class 0-4-2T No 1419 stands in this platform with a Fowey train. This engine was the only one of this type allocated to a Cornish depot at this time, specifically for this duty. There had been two sidings adjacent to this platform until 1946, when two more were added to deal with increasing levels of clay traffic.

On 17 September 2002 No 66146 runs round its Carne Point to Goonbarrow Junction train of empties. The signal box and level crossing can be glimpsed on the left. At one time there was a station footbridge near the box, but this has been removed, as have the attractive down side buildings, demolished in 1976 and replaced by a basic shelter. *Terry Gough/DHM*

LOSTWITHIEL: The Cornwall Railway chose to locate its main workshops here and was the major employer in the town. The buildings were on the up side, south of the station, and adjacent to the River Fowey. A wooden goods shed was provided in a yard close to these workshops and this was still standing on 16 August 1978 as 'Hoover' No 50012 *Benbow* was recorded from a goods dock passing on the 4M05 1245 Penzance to Crewe Perishables and Parcels working.

The goods shed was dismantled in 1982, originally for preservation, but it was subsequently destroyed. Class 50s are no longer in regular service and parcels trains cannot be seen in the Duchy today. The workshop buildings have been used for other business purposes, but have now been converted for residential use. It is still possible to stand on the old goods dock, but the view on 29 May 2006 is somewhat different as No 153373 departs forming the 1720 Newton Abbot to Newquay service. *Both DHM*

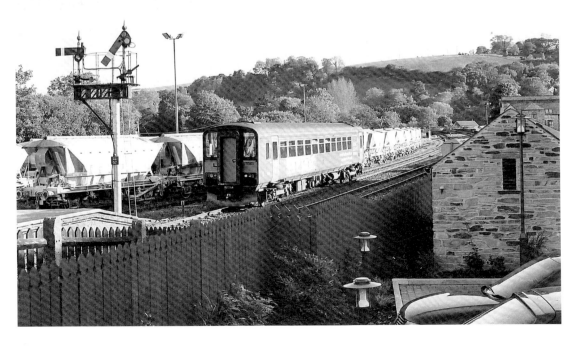

LOSTWITHIEL: The broad gauge Lostwithiel & Fowey Railway opened to goods traffic on 1 June 1869, running for more than 4 miles from Lostwithiel to Carne Point, just north of Fowey. The line was worked and maintained by the Cornwall Railway and initially traffic was heavy. However, the subsequent opening of the Cornwall Mineral Railway's alternative route to Fowey and a depression within the china clay industry had a disastrous effect on the branch's traffic and it was closed on 1 January 1880. Subsequently it was acquired by the CMR, rebuilt to standard gauge and extended to connect with that company's route, re-opening on 16 September 1895. From Lostwithiel, the main line and branch crossed the River Fowey on separate tracks that run parallel for a short distance, and in this 8 August 1959 view from the former, auto-fitted 2-6-2T No 5572 is seen leaving on the 5.5pm to Fowey. The loco is deputising for the usual No 1419.

The independent branch rails over the river were replaced by a new junction in 1972. Standing on the main line in 2006 is not recommended, and in this view from a little further south on 10 April 1984, No 37182 is seen heading for Carne Point to pick up a rake of empty 'clayhoods'. *Peter W. Gray/DHM*

PAR: When opened in 1859, this was merely a through station on the broad gauge Cornwall Railway. It gained in importance in January 1879 when a standard gauge connecting loop was opened from the Cornwall Minerals Railway station at St Blazey. In a scene from a road bridge taken in June 1958, 4-6-0 No 6858 *Woolston Grange* is leaving with an up train as 2-6-2T No 5521 is watered after arriving on a service from Newquay. Just visible on the right is part of the large timber-built goods shed. This was originally the 'tranship shed', which had tracks of the two gauges until 1892, enabling a transfer of goods between them.

The goods yard closed in 1964 and the shed was demolished. The sidings were altered in 1968 for a new Freightliner siding, but this was short-lived and only one siding survives today for engineer's use. On 17 September 2005 No 66237 is about to join the main line with the 6G06 1112 Goonbarrow Junction to Carne Point CDA trip. *Norman Simmons/DHM*

PAR: Looking south from the footbridge at 12.47pm on 2 July 1960, two 4-6-0s, Nos 7820 *Dinmore Manor* and 6837 *Forthampton Grange*, run in with the 13-coach 11.10am (Saturdays only) from Penzance to Birmingham and Wolverhampton. On weekdays this train was 'The Cornishman', but the title was not used on summer Saturdays. Passengers on the down platform are awaiting the 6.50am Paddington to Penzance, which is signalled and will soon arrive behind No 6824 *Ashley Grange*. The station nameboards invite both sets of travellers to 'change for Newquay' and the branch train will soon arrive on the far side of the island platform. A supplement to these signs also advises that passengers for the nearby Carlyon Bay Hotel should also alight here. The 57-lever signal box can be seen above the second loco; it dates from 1890, when it replaced a smaller structure. Originally located off the platform, the main side of the platform was extended beyond the box in 1924. Beyond this is a large water tank that supplied the water columns at each end of the platforms.

The signal box is still in use and controls another pocket of surviving semaphore signalling. It would be most unusual to see a 13-coach train now; more typical is No 150240, which is arriving as the 1012 Penzance to Cardiff service on 9 October 2001. *Peter W. Gray/DHM*

PAR station was largely rebuilt in 1884 to give improved accommodation to suit its new status as a junction. The main buildings are on the down side, and are seen to advantage on Friday 10 September 1971 as Swindon-built Class 42 'Warship' No 827 *Kelly* passes with the 1B15 1230 Paddington to Penzance train; the loco is less than four months from withdrawal. The footbridge once had a roof but it was long gone by this time.

The station is little changed today and the booking office is still open. No 150261 arrives as the 1550 Plymouth to Penzance service on 6 June 2006. *Both DHM*

PAR: In a photo probably taken from the steps of the signal box in June 1958, Hawksworth's 1945-built 4-6-0 No 1008 *County of Cardigan* is on a down passenger train while a '4575' Class 2-6-2T (possibly No 5521) waits with a Newquay departure. The smaller driving wheels on the 'Counties' were considered to be better suited than the 'Castle' Class to the contours of the Cornish main line, while their 'mixed traffic' classification accorded more with the type of work west of Plymouth. A number of this type were based in the Duchy, this loco arriving at Penzance shed from Chester that month.

Two trains disturb the more usual peace on 6 June 2006: No 150244 calls as the 1453 Penzance to Plymouth service, while the 1205 Paddington to Penzance (Nos 43017 and 43189) speeds by. *Norman Simmons/DHM*

PAR: An up refuge siding was located beyond the west end of the station, and in 1925 a carriage siding was laid next to it. Penzance's No 6825 *Llanvair Grange* is seen in the former, some time in the late 1950s. Behind it a goods train is on the up main, and some appreciation can be gained of the 1 in 57 gradient that westbound trains face when they leave Par station. The line continues to climb for more than 6 miles to a summit at Burngullow.

The carriage siding was removed in 1965 but the refuge remains, and is visible on the right as the 0708 'Chopper Topper' railtour from Wolverhampton brings unusual visitors to Cornwall on 31 August 1986. English Electric Type 1s Nos 20124 and 20094 are about to give way to Nos 37235 and 37251, which will 'top and tail' the train to Falmouth and Penzance. The 20s will head the return from there, a first ever visit for the class to mainland Britain's most westerly terminus. *Keith Batchelor collection/DHM*

Looe branch

LISKEARD: The Liskeard & Looe Railway opened from Moorswater to Looe Quay in December 1860, replacing a canal that ran from Moorswater to Terras Pill, south of Sandplace. Because of the difference in height between this railway on the valley floor and the Cornish main line, which crossed it on the viaduct above, it was isolated until 15 May 1901 when a 2-mile connecting loop line was opened between Liskeard and Coombe Junction. This section was steeply graded, much at 1 in 40, and negotiates a horseshoe curve en route. The terminus is at the east end of the main-line station and stands at right angles to it. On 29 September 1959 No 4585 is running round its train after arriving from Looe. The loco is obscuring both a water tower and signal box. To the right is a spacious goods yard and beyond this is the connecting spur with the main line.

Road access to Looe is poor and has helped ensure the branch's survival. No 153374 is about to depart with the 1415 service to Looe on 29 May 2006. The area to the right is now a car park. *Peter W. Gray/DHM*

COOMBE JUNCTION: No 4552 is seen from the steps of the signal box as it arrives with a special working from Liskeard at 5.28pm on 4 July 1959. The steep incline had a speed limit of 15mph in both directions, and can just be noted above the engine's cab, while the front coach is obscuring the line to Looe. The loco will drift into Coombe station, a short distance beyond the box, where it will have to run round before continuing its southward journey. A minor road crosses the railway in the foreground.

The loop adjacent to the halt was taken out of use on 8 May 1981 and the signal box closed; the crossing gates are now user-operated. Freightliner's No 66601 is pictured from the crossing as it completes its descent with a cement train from Earles Sidings, in Derbyshire's Hope Valley, on 30 November 2004. The junction is now operated by train crews under the supervision of the Liskeard signalman, using a ground frame housed in the hut. *Peter W Gray/DHM*

Below The 1901 vintage signal box was photographed on 28 September 1978. *DHM*

COOMBE JUNCTION: The standard gauge Liskeard & Caradon Railway opened from 1844 to 1846 to convey granite, tin and copper to the Liskeard & Looe Union Canal at Moorswater. When the Liskeard & Looe Railway replaced the canal, it was worked by the LCR from 1862, giving a total mileage of more than 19 miles. A passenger service between Moorswater and Looe commenced in September 1879. Mineral traffic north of Moorswater declined in the late 19th century and that section closed on 1 January 1917. When the link line to Liskeard opened, Moorswater station was replaced by one at Coombe. This simple affair can be observed on 8 September 1955 as No 5521 passes with a freight to Liskeard. The large building on the right is Lamellion woollen mill, while Moorswater Viaduct looms in the background.

The station is still open despite the appearance of the heavily overgrown track; but it is one of the least used on today's national network. Only three down and two up trains are booked to call in the current weekday timetable; other services reverse at the junction without trundling the few extra chains to this spot. The mill has been demolished, replaced by a modern unit. *Peter W. Gray/DHM*

COOMBE JUNCTION: Pictured from the minor road bridge just visible beyond the rear of the train on the previous page, No 37142 is ambling along with loaded 'clayhoods' from Moorswater on 28 September 1978. The old canal ran just to the right of the track. Two surviving piers of Brunel's original structure are prominent beside its replacement. A clay works was opened just beyond the viaduct in 1904, with the clay piped in slurry form for more than 4 miles from Parsons Park on Bodmin Moor.

Clay drying ceased in December 1996, but there was some residual traffic for a few months. The line was mothballed, then re-activated in 1999 when a cement distribution depot was established in the works. Initially EWS provided the traction, but Freightliner took over in July 2002. The same view today is almost totally hidden by tree growth, so looking back to 6 April 2000 we find No 37375 on a train of cement empties. There is a second ground frame on the other side of the bridge, enabling a cement train to be 'locked in' and thus not affect the Looe service. *Both DHM*

ST KEYNE station opened on 1 September 1902, about 1½ miles from Coombe Junction. The only intermediate station when the line originally opened was at Causeland, 1½ miles further south, and it was suggested at the time of St Keyne's opening that this under-used facility be closed, but apparently there was sufficient opposition for this not to happen, and indeed it is still open today. St Keyne was built on the site of a limekiln and is pictured in about 1960. The village is a mile to the west, and the nameboard states 'For St Keyne Well', referring to a holy well less than a mile to the south. Brides and their grooms came here, and legend has it that whoever drinks first from the well after the wedding will be master of the house!

An attractive new shelter was erected here in 1997, and it was something of a surprise to find a passenger awaiting No 153372 forming the 1144 Looe to Liskeard service on 29 June 2006. *Author's collection/DHM*

SANDPLACE: The Liskeard & Looe Union Canal opened in 1828 and was primarily built to transport lime, sand and seaweed inland where it was used to combat the local acidic soil, and there were 25 locks in its 6-mile course from Terras Pill to Moorswater. The name of this hamlet is literally derived from where canal barges discharged their cargos of sand and seaweed. When the rest of the canal was abandoned following the building of the railway, a section was retained in use as far as here until 1901. The station was built on a curve adjacent to a bridge over both it and the Looe River, opening in 1881. Just to the south, a loop siding served a local estate from 1879 to 1951. Prairie tank No 4565 is leaving with the 1.23pm Liskeard to Looe train on 15 August 1959.

A new shelter has also been provided here. No 153372 passes by forming the 1245 Looe to Liskeard service on 29 June 2006. This is a request stop, with about two-thirds of trains eligible to call. *Peter W. Gray/DHM*

TERRAS CROSSING: From Sandplace the thick woodland recedes as the valley widens and the East Looe River becomes tidal. Fine panoramas are provided for passengers as the railway runs along the east side of the river on a low embankment/causeway. On 11 July 1959 2-6-2T No 4559 is seen approaching Terras Crossing with the 4.40pm train from Liskeard to Looe. Just this side of the crossing and to the left of the railway was Terras lock, the entry to the canal. Signalling was provided for this minor road crossing in 1902, the only intermediate equipment on the line, but this was modified and a new ground frame installed in 1929. The Liskeard & Looe Railway remained nominally independent until the 1923 grouping, but was worked by the Great Western from 1909. The Prairie tanks were introduced on this line in the 1920s and provided the motive power until services were dieselised from 11 September 1961.

The crossing became ungated in July 1970. The dieselised passenger service has always been provided by units, and visits by locomotives to this branch are now very rare. There was a gorgeous spring evening on Sunday 3 May 1998, with ideal light to witness No 37669 hauling the returning 1Z39 1815 Looe to Cardiff Central 'Cornish Gnome' charter. No 37403 is trailing the consist after providing the power down the branch from Coombe. *Peter W. Gray/DHM*

LOOE: This ancient fishing port comprises two communities on either side of the Looe River estuary, connected by a fine 19th-century bridge of seven low arches. The station is in East Looe, the more important of the twin towns. No 4569 has arrived on the 2.52pm train from Liskeard on 16 August 1960. The track continued past the station to a small goods yard and run-round loop, and, until 1954, beyond that to Buller Quay.

Goods traffic ended in 1963 and the yard was lifted in the following year. In April 1968 the remaining single line was truncated, more than half of the platform removed and the surviving station buildings demolished. No 153372 arrives at what remains, forming the 1215 service from Liskeard on 29 June 2006. A police station has been built across the formation behind the camera. *Derek Frost/DHM*

Around Bodmin General

BODMIN GENERAL: On 2 May 1970 60-year-old veteran 0-6-0ST No 1363 attended an open day at St Blazey. It was worked down to the event on the previous day coupled to D4007 on the Wenford trip. After its appearance, it was piloted back to Bodmin Road by the same loco. Waiting there were two 'Toplight' Brake 3rd coaches, Nos 3755/6, which had been brought down to take part in a film with 1363, the shooting due to take place at Nanstallon Halt. These short (48-foot) and narrow vehicles were built in 1921 for the through GWR City service to Liverpool Street and were later used in other London suburban service; their subsequent survival was due to being used on miners' trains between Glyncorrwg and South Pit Halt in South Wales. The saddle tank is pictured arriving at Bodmin General at 1930 after completing the climb from Bodmin Road. (There was a ban on steam locos working on BR at this time, and this photo is therefore an illusion! Oh, and filming was apparently moved elsewhere due to Cornwall's unpredictable weather!)

Nos 5552 and 4612 pass packed sidings, including the Bodmin & Wenford Railway's diesel fleet, on 3 September 2005. This and the next four 'present' pictures were taken during a steam gala held on that day. *R. A. Lumber/DHM*

BODMIN GENERAL: Looking in the opposite direction from the same road overbridge, the Bodmin Road line is in the foreground as 2-6-2T No 4552 leaves after running round the 12.20pm from there to Wadebridge. The engine shed and water tower can be noted on the left, with the large stone-built goods shed on the right.

A preservation society was formed in 1984, and subsequently the Bodmin & Wenford Railway issued shares in 1985 to purchase the Bodmin Parkway to Boscarne Junction route and track. Regular services between Bodmin Parkway and General commenced in June 1990, with an extension to Boscarne in 1996. A footbridge has been erected next to the narrow road bridge, and in a view therefrom 2-8-0T No 4247 is departing with the 1120 to Boscarne. This engine was based at St Blazey for five years in the 1950s and is therefore a particularly appropriate resident here. *Peter W. Gray/DHM*

BODMIN GENERAL Turning again, but this time looking at the 1888 route to Boscarne, No 08377 is completing the 1 in 40 climb with the daily china clay trip from Wenford on 28 September 1978. The shunter has 12 loaded wagons and a brake-van in tow, and this is believed to have been the limit for the class on this section. A heavier load would have been left at Boscarne Junction to be picked up later by a Class 25 or 37 locomotive. The train will be left in the yard at Lostwithiel, before being taken down the branch to Carne Point.

A former Wenford branch engine, 0-6-0PT No 1369, heads a demonstration goods from Boscarne to Bodmin General. Although it spent more than two years working from Wadebridge shed, this loco would not normally have ventured on this line and would have left any clay traffic at Boscarne for probable collection by a Class 22 loco. It did, however, come this way on 20 February 1965 when it was the last resident BR steam engine in the Duchy, and was en route from Wadebridge to preservation at Totnes. *Both DHM*

BODMIN GENERAL: '4575' Class 2-6-2T No 5539 runs into the station on the 3.24pm train from Wadebridge on 18 March 1961. This type was introduced in 1927, with detail alterations from the preceding '4500' engines, including most obviously their larger-capacity sloping side tanks. The originals were introduced in 1906 and one of these, No 4565, from a 1924 batch, is taking water outside the single-road stone-built engine shed. These classes were ideal for branch-line work and dominated such services in the Duchy. The depot was a sub to St Blazey shed and normally housed a single '45xx' loco overnight.

The shed closed in 1962, but the building survived and in 1969 was leased by the South West Group of the Great Western Society to base its stock, which included ex-GWR 0-6-0ST No 1363 and former Devonport Dockyard Bagnall 0-4-0ST No 19. The former had been purchased in 1964 and had been previously stored at Totnes; while based here it attended three open days at St Blazey, and is pictured after returning home from the last of these on 1 May 1971.

The GWS vacated the premises in 1977 and the shed was unfortunately demolished. The conical 30-foot-high overhead water tank was, however, preserved by the Society and moved to its centre at Didcot on a 'Weltrol' wagon. The site of the shed is on the right of the third view, taken on 16 August 1980; No 37142 has just run round the 0700 'Pixilated Pixie' charter from Cheltenham and is about to venture down to Boscarne.

The Bodmin & Wenford Railway has erected a two-road shed at this spot; 2-8-0T No 4247 is passing on the 1445 service from Bodmin Parkway. On the left a pair of Wenford branch stalwarts, Nos 1369 and 30587, are coupled together. *Peter W. Gray/J. F. Medley/R. A. Lumber/DHM*

BODMIN GENERAL station stands on high ground a few hundred yards to the south of the town centre, and received the 'General' suffix in September 1949. Prairie No 4565 has arrived on the 9am train from Padstow on 25 August 1960 and is running round before continuing to Bodmin Road. The signal box was located adjacent to the ramp at the far end of the single platform, and can just be seen to the right of the train. On the left is the substantial goods shed, built of local stone.

General goods traffic ceased in May 1967 and the signal box closed on 17 December of that year. Both it and the goods shed were demolished in the 1970s, but the stone-built main station building was leased while the Wenford traffic kept the station on the railway map, and has thus survived into the preservation era. 2-8-0T No 4247 has just arrived with the 1545 train from Boscarne, while 2-6-2T No 5552 stands next to the water tank. On the left the Port of Par's *Alfred* can just be glimpsed in front of the locomotive workshop. A signal box has been erected on the site of the original, and the apex of its roof can be glimpsed above the first coach. *R. A. Lumber/DHM*

Routes to Fowey

GOLANT: After the Lostwithiel & Fowey Railway's line was re-opened under the auspices of the Cornwall Mineral Railway in 1895, it was to suffer further periods of closure during both World Wars due to restrictions on coastal shipping and military occupation of the area. These closures lasted for seven months in 1917, and there were three periods totalling more than 2½ years without trains in the years from 1940 to 1944. The branch hugs the west bank of the River Fowey for most of its way and the only easy access by road is at the village of Golant, where the line crosses the tiny harbour on a causeway. '1400' Class 0-4-2T No 1468 is propelling its auto-trailer from Fowey to Lostwithiel in the early afternoon of 3 April 1961. It has just left the only intermediate station on the line, a simple halt that opened on 1 July 1896.

The only way that the public can enjoy this delightful journey today is by travelling on one of the very occasional charters that traverse the branch. On 29 May 2006 No 37411 is heading the returning 'Fowey Pony' from Carne Point. *Peter W. Gray/DHM*

FOWEY: The standard gauge Cornwall Mineral Railway had its origin in a number of horse-worked railways built by Joseph Thomas Treffry. The CMR was empowered to purchase these tramways, convert them for locomotive haulage and build additional lines; the new railway opened for goods traffic on 1 June 1874. This new system ran from Newquay on Cornwall's north coast through the heart of china clay country to Fowey on the south coast of the peninsula, with other lines in between. The brand new extension from Par to Fowey gave direct access to the deep-water port at Fowey, the site of a medieval naval base but a port that had never developed to its true potential due to poor accessibility. The CMR built three jetties north of the town for the opening of its line, and a passenger service from Fowey to Newquay commenced on 20 June 1876. However, the railway struggled financially and the whole of the then extant CMR system was worked by the Great Western from October 1877, and amalgamated with that company on 1 July 1896. Four additional jetties were opened that year, with an eighth following in 1923. As previously mentioned, the CMR's route was connected with the branch from Lostwithiel in 1895.

The station was built on a curve adjacent to Caffamill Pill. Passenger traffic on the Fowey to St Blazey section was never heavy and the service was withdrawn on 8 July 1929, although unadvertised workmen's trains ran until December 1934. Other than the aforementioned wartime breaks, passenger trains did continue to operate from Lostwithiel to Fowey, and one such train is seen approaching the single platform behind 0-4-2T No 1419 in June 1958. On the left 2-8-0T No 4248 is waiting to gain access to the docks with a loaded china clay train from St Blazey. This platform was the original CMR one, but another one (and third line) had been sited to the left of the clay train from 1895 to 1951.

This passenger service was withdrawn on 4 January 1965. With a need to invest in the dock infrastructure and also improve road access, an agreement was reached between BR and the English China Clay Company whereby the former agreed to close the line from St Blazey to Par and lease the trackbed, which would be converted into a private road for the exclusive use of ECC lorries. The company also leased the whole of the dock complex from here to Carne Point. In exchange, minimum annual tonnage guarantees were given to BR for rail traffic that would arrive there via Lostwithiel. The line to St Blazey closed from 1 July 1968, and the station site is shown in May 2006.

The third photo was taken on 26 September 1970 and shows an interim period: the road can be seen on the right, but there was also still one track running past the old station. This was subsequently removed and the railway now ends adjacent to No 8 jetty, more than half a mile from this spot. The loco is D3476, one of three Class 10 shunters acquired from BR to work the docks. *Norman Simmons/DHM(2)*

PINNOCK TUNNEL: From Fowey the Par line climbed at 1 in 36/40 for more than a mile to this tunnel, at 1,173 yards the longest in Cornwall. It was bored through granite, working from both ends and from five shafts along its course. In a picture from the cab of 2-8-0T No 4273 on 23 September 1960, a train of empties from the docks is approaching the tunnel. From 1908 until 1958 a small six-lever signal box stood just beyond the timber hut on the right. Beyond the tunnel the line descended at 1 in 50 towards Par. Heavy loaded trains coming in the opposite direction were worked bunker first with the chimney behind the crew, as otherwise there was a risk of asphyxiation in the confines of the tunnel.

When the route was converted to a road, the formation was widened to provide for two lanes, but access through the tunnel is one lane only by necessity, and is controlled by traffic lights. Lighting was also installed within, and doors at the west end can be closed to allow extractor fans to ventilate the tunnel of fumes. The east end was recorded during an official RCTS visit on a wet day in April 1997. *R. C. Riley/DHM*

PAR BRIDGE: The descent from Pinnock ended at Par Sands, where the line then ran in a westerly direction along the back of the beach, before turning northwards and passing under the main line to the west of Par station. Shortly afterwards it joined the Par Harbour branch, then passed over Par Bridge level crossing. No 4248 has just crossed the A3082 and is heading for Fowey with a loaded china clay train from St Blazey in June 1958. The crossing was controlled from the signal box that is just visible above the first wagon. The line to Par Harbour is in the foreground. St Blazey shed normally had an allocation of at least two of these 2-8-0Ts, with their primary duty being the Fowey line. Depending on the number of sailings, about six trains a day could operate each way over this route. Trains were allowed about 25 minutes for the 4-mile journey down to the docks, but would have to stop to pin down the wagon brakes before descending from Pinnock.

No 08955 approaches the crossing on 7 February 1993 after leaving wagons at Par Harbour for loading. *Norman Simmons/DHM*

PAR BRIDGE: Viewed from the north side of the crossing on 8 September 1955, '5700' Class 0-6-0PT No 3635 is about to pass St Blazey shed while heading a trip working from Par Harbour to St Blazey yard. The signal box is just to the south of the crossing, but is hidden by the front van. The left-hand semaphore on the bracket is for the Fowey route, while the lower one controls the line to the Port of Par.

The signal box closed with the Fowey route in 1968. The crossing gates are now manually operated by the travelling shunter on the infrequent trips down to Par Harbour. The location was visited by the Branch Line Society's 'Cornishman' tour on 4 May 1986, but Laira's Class 118 DMU No P460 was not permitted past these gates. The unit had been given a British Telecom yellow livery for advertising purposes the previous year. *Peter W. Gray/DHM*

PAR HARBOUR: The aforementioned Joseph Treffry was a prominent landowner who planned to develop the harbour at Fowey to serve his mining interests, but was defeated by other landowners who would not allow him to extend his tramway there. He was also unable to obtain better rates from the owners of Charlestown Harbour, so instead purchased land near Par with the intention of building an artificial harbour, which received its first vessel in 1833. A canal was built from the harbour to connect with the terminus of his tramway at Ponts Mill, north of St Blazey. In 1855 the canal was replaced by a horse-drawn tramway built alongside it. As with the other sections of Treffry's tramways, this route was rebuilt to form part of the Cornwall Minerals Railway. The harbour had its own internal railway system, and on 10 September 1971 0-4-0ST *Alfred* is using the branch as a headshunt while shunting loaded clay wagons. Beyond it is Five Arches bridge, which had also once crossed the Fowey line to the right.

The 0730 Paddington to Penzance HST (Nos 43169 and 43088) is seen on this bridge on 6 June 2006. *Both DHM*

PAR HARBOUR became an important centre for both drying and shipping china clay. A tidal harbour, it is used by smaller coastal vessels that work to UK and cross-Channel ports handling cargoes of up to 3,000 tonnes, whereas the deep-water port at Fowey has tended to load larger ocean-going ships with up to 12,000 tonnes. An extensive railway system was developed to cater for all the activity here, and saddle tank *Alfred* is pictured again with a rake of clay wagons on 10 September 1971.

Steam operation ceased in 1977 and the rail network within the harbour has been considerably reduced. The St Blazey pilot occasionally potters down to the remaining sidings with the odd wagon or two, and any internal shunting is performed by a road tractor. On 22 April 1997 a ferry wagon is being loaded with bagged clay as the rain lashes down. On the left is the large 'Cambrian' bulk clay store, while the former SR utility van on the right was being used by the ECC employees' model railway society. The connection to the private road to Fowey is behind the camera. Currently more than 200 men still work here, but in July 2006 it was announced that activity will be severely curtailed. By late 2007 it is planned that all sea shipments will cease, with only a limited amount of clay drying then undertaken on site. However, it is understood that rail shipments will continue from here. *Both DHM*

PAR HARBOUR: Another 1971 view shows *Alfred* moving about the system. The main line between Par (three-quarters of a mile to the left) and St Austell is in the foreground, and until 1965 there had been another connection from this line into the harbour, to the right of this scene, controlled by Par Harbour signal box. A branch from the harbour passed below the box to serve the now abandoned kilns on Par Moor. It was the restricted headroom under this bridge that dictated the cut-down design of the Port's *Alfred* and sister engine *Judy*. The two 0-4-0STs were built by W. G. Bagnall Ltd in 1953 and 1937 respectively, and happily both have been preserved. *DHM*

The second view shows *Alfred* again as it slowly approaches its tiny engine shed after an appearance at the St Blazey open day on 3 May 1969. *R. A. Lumber*

ST BLAZEY SHED: The CMR established its headquarters in St Blazey, with facilities including offices, substantial workshops and a semi-roundhouse built of Devonshire brick in 1873. The CMR locomotive stock comprised 18 Sharp Stewart 0-6-0Ts designed to work in pairs, back-to-back, and each of the shed's nine roads was able to accommodate one pair. When the GWR started to work the CMR, it retained nine of these locos and rebuilt them as saddle tanks. Although they subsequently strayed elsewhere on the system, there was usually one of the class at St Blazey until 1924. More typical residents of 83E in later steam years are pannier tanks Nos 1627 and 8713, but both were only allocated here for a short time, thus dating this photo to about September 1959.

The shed closed to steam in April 1962, but the roundhouse remained in use as a diesel depot until final closure on 24 April 1987. Following repairs and the construction of internal walls, each bay of this listed building is now used as an industrial unit. The fenced-off turntable is still in use and is just to the left of this 2006 view. *Keith Batchelor collection/DHM*

ST BLAZEY SHED: This view from about 1958 includes three of the classes of loco most closely associated with the depot. Next to the turntable is 2-8-0T No 4294 with a '4575' Class 2-6-2T behind, while 0-6-0PT No 8702 is next to the combined water tank/coal stage erected by the GWR in 1896. St Blazey provided locos for the china clay lines and the local passenger branches, and its allocation was therefore dominated by tank engines. Its limited main-line turns were covered by about half a dozen 4-6-0s, usually 'Granges' and 'Halls'. *Norman Simmons*

The depot did not have an allocation of main-line locos in diesel days, but the open day on 1 May 1971 sees typical power of the time in the shape of Class 42 'Warship' No 806 *Cambrian* on the left, with a Class 43 version No 854 *Tiger* in the shed. Less typical is 'star turn' 0-6-0ST No 1363, which is on the vacuum-operated turntable (hence the large cylinders). However, this 1910 design was based on the original Sharp Stewart engines, and although the class were mainly intended for dock shunting, there was often one at St Blazey in their early years for use on the Goonbarrow branch. *John Medley*

St Blazey to St Dennis Junction

ST BLAZEY: The CMR's station here was named Par until December 1878, shortly before the opening of the connecting loop to the Cornwall Railway's own Par station. Evidently there was little demand for it, as it closed in September 1925, although workmen's services continued until 1934. The platforms remain today and the down one is clearly visible behind 'Warship' No 806 *Cambrian* on 1 May 1971. The double-track Par loop is in the foreground, while the rails on the left lead to the shed. The siding on the right is one of two added in 1924, and marks the approximate position of the original CMR signal box. The sidings behind its 1908 replacement date from about 1910; a footbridge was erected at that time to span the sidings and link the two platforms.

Scrap metal traffic is currently being loaded in the sidings behind the box. Photographed from a public footpath, No 153373 forms the 1124 Par to Newquay service on 6 June 2006. *John Medley/DHM*

ST BLAZEY: The 1315 Newquay to Bodmin Road DMU pauses (but not for passengers) at 1403 on Saturday 2 May 1970. Beyond the 41-lever signal box is the original CMR station building, its brickwork by now rendered; it was demolished not long afterwards.

Turning the other way on 24 October 1998, an official RCTS visit to the still operational signal box happily coincided with the running of the 1Z30 0728 Paddington to Newquay 'Royal Duchy' railtour, hauled by a pair of ex-LMS locos, 8F 2-8-0 No 48773 and 'Black 5' 4-6-0 No 45110. There was also some reprieve in the weather, when the day's torrential rain eased sufficiently to record the locos while they were stopped for water. *R. A. Lumber/DHM*

MIDDLEWAY BRIDGE CROSSING: Just 12 chains north of St Blazey signal box a small cabin was provided by the GWR to protect the crossing over a road from St Blazey to Par. The River Par ran immediately in front of the box and its rods and wires had to span the river before reaching the single track. Perhaps surprisingly for a not particularly busy line, a substantial wooden footbridge also once spanned both the railway and river here, but this was removed in the 1930s. The 7-lever box can be noted on the left as No 47492 passes with the 0845 SO Newquay to Manchester service on 6 September 1980. The alignment of the old Ponts Mill to Par Harbour canal is in the foreground.

   The box closed in the following year, and automatic barriers with CCTV are now controlled from St Blazey box. No 153373 forms the 1017 Newquay to Par service on 6 June 2006. Note that the semaphores have been moved further from the crossing on both sides. *R. A. Lumber/DHM*

MIDDLEWAY BRIDGE CROSSING: 0-6-0PT No 1664 trundles towards the crossing with the return working of the Goonbarrow branch goods on 13 July 1961. The railway appears to run on a causeway here with the river, white with clay waste, in the foreground and the old canal on the other side of the formation. All of this area was once under the sea, but centuries of mining and silting up have moved the shoreline some 2 miles to the south.

Pictured a little further to the north, past and present came together on 30 August 2002 when preserved Class 52 No D1015 *Western Champion* worked a scheduled freight as part of a crew training exercise. Although this class worked clay trains prior to their final withdrawal in 1977, they would not have hauled the CDA wagons that formed the 6G10 1550 Goonbarrow Junction to Carne Point. Environmental concerns mean that the river now has a more natural look! *Peter W. Gray/DHM*

TREFFRY VIADUCT: Treffry's standard gauge horse-drawn tramway from Ponts Mill to Molinnis, near Bugle, was opened in May 1847 to serve several granite quarries and china clay works. The tramway ascended the side of the Luxulyan Valley at an average gradient of 1 in 10, by means of a 947-yard-long inclined plane known as Carmears Incline. It was rope-worked by a water-wheel and rose 325 feet in height. Three-quarters of a mile beyond the incline, the tramway then crossed the valley on a magnificent viaduct that is also an aqueduct – a water trough beneath the rails carried the water used to power the water-wheel. The 10-arch granite viaduct is 216 yards long and 98 feet high. When the CMR rebuilt the tramway, a new line was built in the valley avoiding the incline, and this runs beneath the viaduct. Looking down therefrom on 19 June 1956, a pair of pannier tanks are slowly descending Luxulyan bank with a clay train.

A public footpath now crosses the structure and the 1322 Newquay to Paddington HST is seen on 17 September 2005. *Hugh Davies/DHM*

LUXULYAN: Viewed from a road bridge just south of the station in 1958, 0-6-0PT No 1626 is completing its 1 in 37 climb of Luxulyan bank with what is probably the Goonbarrow branch goods comprising in the main about 28 empty clay wagons. Exhaust can be seen from a banking engine behind the brake-van, but the loco is hidden by the flora. The banker will possibly be cut off here and may then recess in the refuge siding on the right. The latter is on the alignment of the original tramway, which until 1933 still saw occasional traffic from Colcerrow Quarry, on the far side of the viaduct. A gate is just visible – this marked the extent of horse working from the quarry. The 13-tonne wooden-bodied clay wagons were built at Swindon in the 1950s and are descended from a 1913 design.

In today's heavily overgrown scene, the rear of the train seen on page 112 is about to start its descent. The air-braked CDA hoppers were introduced on services to Carne Point in 1988 when they replaced their vacuum-braked predecessors. *Norman Simmons/DHM*

LUXULYAN: Looking in the opposite direction from the same bridge on 8 July 1961, 4-6-0 No 6875 *Hindford Grange* is seen leaving the station on the 11.52am Newquay to Par train. 'Bridges for Luxulyan' station opened in June 1876 when passenger services commenced over the CMR's line from Newquay to Fowey. Originally there were two short conventional platforms, but these were replaced by a longer island platform in 1910. The small station building can be noted to the left of the cottage. The chimney on the right belongs to Treskilling china clay works, which opened in 1916 and was served by a siding from the goods yard.

Only the cottage really identifies this as being the same location on 6 June 2006 as No 66002 passes with the 6G06 Goonbarrow Junction to Carne Point china clay train. During a time of reducing numbers of clay trains, this was the most regular CDA working, but still could not be relied upon to work every day. *Peter W. Gray/DHM*

LUXULYAN: In a June 1958 view from tracks leading to the goods yard on the left, 0-6-0PT No 9755 is in the down platform with a goods train. The signal box dated from 1911 when it replaced a CMR structure located a little to the south. Beyond the box a clerestory roofed camping coach can be glimpsed; enthusiasts staying here are just about to board the 'Toad' brake-van. A 'pagoda' waiting shelter is located on the platform.

The signal box closed in September 1964 when all the trackwork was taken out of use apart from the main running line and a siding to the works, which survived until 1975. The platform is now provided with a basic hut, but this is not visible in today's cluttered scene with the site of the goods yard covered with rubble and old track sections. *Norman Simmons/DHM*

GOONBARROW JUNCTION: Located about half a mile from Bugle, this was originally Rosevear Junction, where a line diverged to serve Rosevear china clay kiln. The CMR opened the Goonbarrow branch from this junction to serve a number of clay kilns to the south in October 1893. Over the years the site expanded as sidings were added and a number of spurs provided to serve kilns in the immediate vicinity of the junction. A new signal box was provided in about 1909, replacing the original CMR installation. This is pictured in the late 1950s with the Newquay branch in the foreground; the double track section has commenced to the left. In the sidings behind, 0-6-0PT No 1626 has brought a train off the Goonbarrow branch. The prominent chimney belongs to Wheal Henry kiln.

In a 22 April 1997 view from behind the signal box, No 37668 is in a similar position to the pannier tank, and is about to depart for Carne Point. The rear of its train is on a remaining stub of the Goonbarrow branch. The shortened Wheal Henry stack is just to the left. *Norman Simmons/DHM*

GOONBARROW JUNCTION signal box still controls the only passing loop on the branch with semaphore signals, and this location is now the northern limit of china clay traffic on the line. In a scene from just in front of the box on 24 October 1998, the signalman is exchanging tokens with the driver of No 153308, forming the 1203 service from Newquay to Par. *Both DHM*

About a third of a mile of the Goonbarrow branch remains in use today as a headshunt for traffic from Rocks dryers. No 37668 is seen again as it runs round on this section in April 1997. Wheal Henry siding is on the left; its kiln closed in the 1960s but the siding is still available for shunting purposes. Rocks produces filler clays for the paper industry and is now the sole remaining loading point for traffic at this location. Most of the output is moved by rail and production could actually increase here as part of the proposed changes within the industry. *DHM*

GOONBARROW JUNCTION: In July 1930 the line was doubled from east of the signal box to west of Bugle station, a distance of about a mile. The box is visible in the distance as two trains meet on this section in June 1958: 0-6-0PT No 9655 and 2-6-2T No 5519 are waiting for the road with an up goods, as another Prairie tank, No 5521, approaches on a train for Newquay. It was normal practice for the local tank engines to be facing in this direction so that they would work chimney first up the prevailing gradients. The vans on the left are on the up refuge siding. The two tracks to the right of the down main are sidings, with the Goonbarrow branch on the right; all these rails have received a liberal coating of 'white gold'.

In a 3 September 1994 view looking to the right of the 'past' scene, the Goonbarrow branch headshunt is now in the left foreground, with the rails to Rocks dryers curving away to the right; a rake of CDA hoppers can be glimpsed in the reception siding. *Norman Simmons/DHM*

116

BUGLE: Treffry's 1847 tramway from Ponts Mill terminated at a clay-loading wharf at Molinnis, not far from the Bugle Inn; its name was derived from the bugle in the badge of the Cornish Regiment, whose soldiers frequented the coaching inn. The village grew around the inn, with rapid growth in the late 19th century as the clay industry expanded. The exact location of the terminus is not known, but it was probably just to the west of Molinnis Crossing on the later CMR. When the track from Goonbarrow Junction was doubled in 1930, a new 41-lever signal box was provided adjacent to this crossing. The signalman is leaning out of the box to speak to the driver of No 5502, on a train for Newquay in June 1958.

The box was reduced to a ground frame when the passenger line was singled on 29 November 1964, and closed totally in August 1973. There is now a 5mph speed limit for trains over the crossing, which is ungated and has warning lights activated by approaching trains. *Norman Simmons/DHM*

BUGLE: When the passenger service between Newquay and Fowey started in 1876, a station was located here with a signal box just off the east end of the platform. An island platform was provided during the 1930 doubling, with access from a road overbridge, and the CMR box was replaced by the one seen on the previous page. Although the down passenger line has been removed, the station is substantially intact on 2 May 1970 as the 1115 Bodmin Road to Newquay DMU calls, but there does appear to be a distinct lack of custom. The signal box and crossing can be glimpsed in the distance. The two-siding up goods yard to the left was closed in 1964. The line on the right is the branch to Carbis Wharf, but by this time it was worked as an independent route from Goonbarrow Junction.

The platform survives but can barely be seen on 3 September 2005 as an HST passes. The foreground is now heavily overgrown, with new housing erected on both sides of the line. *R. A. Lumber/DHM*

BUGLE: Viewed from the other side of the road bridge on a glorious 28 April 1962, 2-6-2Ts Nos 4564 and 5531 are propelling the Plymouth Railway Circle's 'Cornwall Mineral' brake-van special at the start of their short journey down the Carbis Wharf branch. The track curving to the left in the foreground is the Wheal Rose branch, which was only half a mile long but still served several china clay works. A proposal to extend this line to Carbis proved impractical, so the separate branch was built. The track to the left of the brake-vans forms part of a loop, while steam is obscuring the end of the double-track section on the Newquay line. This was the final steam working from St Blazey shed, although these engines and No 5518 were stored there as spares until September 1963, and provided a welcome playground for the author and his friends!

The foreground is now heavily overgrown, so a position to the right was selected on 3 September 2005 to witness the 1126 Newquay to Paddington HST (Nos 43185 and 43022) on the single remaining line. *Peter W. Gray/DHM*

119

ROCHE: When the CMR system opened, a depot named Holywell was provided here, there being a holy well in the locality. At the commencement of the passenger service in 1876, the station was named Victoria after a nearby inn. It finally gained its present name on 1 May 1904, after the village about a mile to the south. The name is derived from the French for 'rock', and refers to the area's landmark, a 100-foot-high granite crag rising from the plateau on which the village stands. Surmounting the rock are the ruins of a small chapel with a hermit's cell. The station is pictured from the down platform in an undated view that shows the main building and 24-lever signal box on the opposite side. The small goods yard is to the right, on the up side.

The box closed in January 1965 when the down platform line and all the sidings were taken out of use; six months later the down line was re-instated in lieu of the up platform loop. Current access to the remaining platform is via a foot crossing at the west end. *Lens of Sutton Association/DHM*

NEAR ROCHE: The 600-foot summit of the line is to the west of Roche, and Nos 7816 *Frilsham Manor* and 6832 *Brockton Grange* have nearly completed their 1 in 40 climb to this summit at 12.55pm on 19 July 1958 with the 14-coach 12.30 SO Newquay to Paddington train. The road bridge in the centre of the photo carries the B3274, while just visible on the extreme left is the low girder bridge over the A30. Beyond this the wilds of Goss Moor stretch into the distance; the railway and trunk road parallel one another for about 3 miles across it. Much of the line on this section was double track from 1921 to 1965.

The steel A30 bridge replaced a wooden one in 1930, and has a 14ft 3in headroom. Over the years it has become a notorious accident black spot and, despite ample warning, has been regularly hit by lorries whose drivers apparently either cannot read or don't know the height of their own vehicles! For many years there were proposals to build a new road along the railway formation, with rail services to Newquay diverted via Burngullow and a re-instated section of line between Parkandillick and St Dennis Junction; however, work on a new dual carriageway to the north was being undertaken on 6 June 2006, when No 153373 was working the 0813 Plymouth to Newquay service. *Peter W. Gray/DHM*

ST DENNIS JUNCTION: Treffry's tramway from Newquay to Hendra passed this spot from 1849, but the site became Bodmin Road Junction in 1874 with the opening of the CMR's Par to Newquay line and its branches to Melangoose Mill (Retew branch) and Drinnick Mill (an extension from Hendra Crazey). The location was renamed in 1878, and although the latter line had closed as far as Parkandillick in 1966, the Retew branch was still nominally open and much of the junction infrastructure intact on 1 August 1981 as No 47199 passed at 1630 on the 1055 SO Paddington to Newquay train.

The Retew Branch was officially closed in the following April, but the passing loop on the Newquay branch was retained until the signal box closed on 14 December 1986. The junction then provided access to engineers' spoil sidings, but the connection was severed by removing a length of track in February 1992. Nos 43123 and 43097 power the 0825 SO Edinburgh to Newquay HST on 25 July that year.

The disused track was soon removed and the site was to be transformed from the following year when work started on the Indian Queens by-pass; the A30 now crosses the bridge seen behind No 153373 rather than the one from which these photos were taken. The 1327 Par to Newquay service was recorded on 6 June 2006. Enough room was left under the new bridge to accommodate the proposed diversion of the Newquay branch previously referred to. *All DHM*

The final photo depicts a lengthy train of china clay empties from St Blazey, which has arrived next to the signal box in June 1958 and is bound for the Retew branch. Power is provided by 2-8-0T No 4294 and 2-6-2T No 5519, although the former would not be permitted to run down the branch. The other lines radiating from this location will receive coverage in the forthcoming volume in this series on West Cornwall. *Norman Simmons*

Goonbarrow branch

GUNHEATH: The CMR opened this 3½-mile branch from Goonbarrow Junction on 2 October 1893 with the aim of serving a number of china clay works. Although the rest of the CMR system was being worked by the GWR at this time, the new line was operated by its owners until the whole system was amalgamated with the GWR in 1896. A Peckett 0-6-0ST *Goonbarrow* was ordered to work the branch and was based on the line in a shed at Stenalees. At different times 11 different sidings were served beyond the immediate Goonbarrow Junction area, including Gunheath, about 3 miles from the junction. A pannier tank, probably No 1626, is seen shunting clay wagons adjacent to the loading wharf in about 1958. The line from the junction is running in on the right after a 1 in 39 descent; the extension to Carbean is in the foreground. The clay pit can be glimpsed in the background.

The cottages visible on the right of the 'past' scene have gone, and the area today forms part of the enlarged pit. The dirt track in the right foreground follows the route of the railway. *Norman Simmons/DHM*

CARBEAN: To reach the terminus, trains had to reverse at Gunheath then descend at a steep gradient of 1 in 35. Due to this grade, the engine would lead the train down and propel it up the incline. 0-6-0PT No 1626 is pictured with its 'Toad' brake-van on 18 June 1958. The two figures to its right are standing on the loading wharf, while further right is the main A391 Bodmin to St Austell road. Due to clearance restrictions and track curvature, only short-wheelbase locos were allowed on this line.

Traffic on this section had petered out by 1963, and the last 2 miles of the branch closed on 29 April 1965. Other than the foreground access 'road' it is difficult to reconcile the two pictures, but the main road is just beyond the bushes on the right. *David Lawrence/DHM*

Carbis Wharf branch

ROSEMELLYN: This line was opened by the CMR in June 1874 at the same time as its main Fowey to Newquay route, and was only just over a mile long. About half way along the branch it met a minor road at Rosemellyn level crossing, and the gates can be noted in the distance behind the Branch Line Society's 'Cornishman' tour of 4 May 1986, one of only a handful of passenger specials that traversed this freight-only line during its existence. The tour was unable to proceed beyond this point due to the state of the waterlogged track beneath a road overbridge behind the camera. The stack of the long-closed Rosemellyn Clay Works is visible to the left of the DMU. A siding served this works from shortly after the line's opening until 1948.

The September 2005 view was taken from the right of the field visible on the extreme right of the 'past' photo, and thus also includes the still standing stack. The line of trees on the left marks the route of the branch. *Both DHM*

CARBIS WHARF: The PRC's 'Cornwall Mineral' special of 28 April 1962 is seen again as Nos 4564 and 5531 gingerly propel the 11 brake-vans for the final few yards towards the terminus. There were two roads here and the special is taking the left-hand one, which handled clay traffic from the adjacent Great Wheal Prosper Kiln. The other siding served a general wharf where clay and other merchandise was handled. The layout was too restricted to provide a run-round loop and trains were always propelled down the line. Roche Rock can be seen on the horizon.

After 1967 the only traffic on the branch was from Great Wheal Prosper, and this dwindled to only one monthly wagonload of clay. This amount of traffic did not justify any work on the deteriorating track and the final such wagon left here in August 1989. The works continued for a while, but were subsequently closed and sold. During 2005 the building was converted into dwelling accommodation offering bed and breakfast facilities. *Peter W. Gray/DHM*

INDEX OF LOCATIONS